WE NEED YOUR ART

WE NEED YOUR ART

Stop F*cking Around and Make Something

AMIE McNEE

Ebury Press

UK | USA | Canada | Ireland | Australia
India | New Zealand | South Africa

Ebury Press is part of the Penguin Random House group of companies
whose addresses can be found at global.penguinrandomhouse.com

Penguin Random House UK
One Embassy Gardens, 8 Viaduct Gardens, London SW11 7BW

penguin.co.uk
global.penguinrandomhouse.com

First published in the USA by Penguin Life in 2025
First published in the United Kingdom by Ebury Press in 2025

4

Copyright © Amie McNee 2025
Illustrations copyright © Amie McNee 2025

The moral right of the author has been asserted.

Penguin Random House values and supports copyright. Copyright fuels creativity, encourages diverse voices, promotes freedom of expression and supports a vibrant culture. Thank you for purchasing an authorised edition of this book and for respecting intellectual property laws by not reproducing, scanning or distributing any part of it by any means without permission. You are supporting authors and enabling Penguin Random House to continue to publish books for everyone. No part of this book may be used or reproduced in any manner for the purpose of training artificial intelligence technologies or systems. In accordance with Article 4(3) of the DSM Directive 2019/790, Penguin Random House expressly reserves this work from the text and data mining exception.

Designed by Nerylsa Dijol

Printed and bound in Great Britain by Clays Ltd, Elcograf S.p.A.

The authorised representative in the EEA is Penguin Random House Ireland,
Morrison Chambers, 32 Nassau Street, Dublin D02 YH68

A CIP catalogue record for this book is available from the British Library

ISBN 9781529937015

Penguin Random House is committed to a sustainable future for our business, our readers and our planet. This book is made from Forest Stewardship Council® certified paper.

To James.
My beloved. My creative collaborator.
This book is as much yours as it is mine.
Thanks for letting me have all the glory.

CONTENTS

Introduction ix

ACT ONE // **THE CASE FOR CREATIVITY** 1

Art: Responsible, Important, Sensible 3

Art Heals 19

ACT TWO // **YOU ARE THE ARTIST** 27

Coronate Yourself 29

Small Magic 43

The Two-Week Reset Challenge 53

ACT THREE // **BLOCKS** 67

On Procrastination 69

On Perfectionism 84

On Jealousy and Comparison 101

On Burnout 118

ACT FOUR // **BUILDING AN ABUNDANT PRACTICE** *139*

    On Voice *141*

    On Self-Censorship *154*

    On Finishing *177*

    On Failure *195*

    On Success *211*

    On Patience *226*

    On Celebrating *241*

Conclusion 250
Acknowledgements 253
Resources 255

WE NEED YOUR ART

INTRODUCTION

We need your art.

I envision you picking up this book, reading the title and squinting at it with deep suspicion. 'My art? Who needs my art?'

We do. The world does.

'The world needs *my* art?' you ask incredulously.

Your art. We, the people, need YOUR art.

'But why?'

So glad you asked. I wrote a whole book about it. Let's begin.

Most of us have had, at some time, an inkling that there is something more – that we have something to give, to make, to create. Perhaps you have a glimmer of an idea for a novel or a bizarre pull toward watercolour paints. Maybe every time you watch a good movie you feel overcome with a grief that you weren't a part of its creation.

You are made to create, but it's so hard to detach and rewrite the stories we have been sold about what we are meant to be doing with our lives. Many of the systems we're forced to participate in smother our creative fire; some don't even let us light the match. We're told that in order to be responsible, we need to focus on the serious stuff. The adult stuff. Not that art stuff. Not that making stuff. Many of us wouldn't dare lay claim to the title 'Artist'. That word is for a special group of people. Not you, not me, right?

Screw* these stories.

---

*I have a proclivity for swearing, and my favourite curse word is *fuck*. In the first draft of this book, the word appeared 130 times. However, to account for different tastes in profanity, we have opted to use the word *screw* instead within the text. But please know that every time you read the word *screw*, I mean *fuck*.

YOU HAVE BEEN SEDUCED INTO BELIEVING YOU ARE INCONSEQUENTIAL. IT IS A LIE. WE NEED YOU. WE NEED YOUR ART.

INTRODUCTION

I believe you are on this planet to make art. I believe we all are. Making art is the ultimate human act. The impulse to create is instinctual, untaught, innate to us as a species. I could talk (and I do) to literally anyone and discover that somehow, somewhere, even under the most debilitating circumstances, they are currently creating something or have an idea about something they want to make. Denying art is denying your nature. The act of creation makes a better version of you. It gives you purpose, agency and challenge. It demands that you explore the caverns of who you are and discover what lives within – the beautiful and the messy.

You are on this planet to make art. Not just for yourself but for the world. Because it needs your art. Humans rely on the arts to inspire, to take refuge, to challenge, to awaken. Communities flourish when artists live within them. Once more: you are on this planet to make art. Spreading that simple idea has been my mission for the past decade.

For a long time, I wanted to tell stories. But I held the shameful belief that making art was frivolous, irresponsible and embarrassing – that I should probably keep my hopes to myself. Still, I wrote. And as I told my stories, something changed within me. Writing connected me to joy, to ambition, to rebellion and delight. These silly little stories were giving me purpose.

It took a few more years of deconstructing my creative shame to realise this feeling of purpose is precisely the magic of art. Creating gives us agency, it gives us control, it gives us delight. The bizarre external forces of the world no longer batter us, or at least don't batter us quite so much. When we create, we become the author, the maker, the god of our own little artist realm.

I'm not alone in the realisation that art is deeply important for individuals and crucial for communities and society as a whole. Study after study from pioneering researchers like Daisy Fancourt and Maria Rosario Jackson show the overwhelmingly positive impact of the arts. Creating art consistently not only increases happiness but also reduces negative affect and makes us feel more satisfied. I'll get into the research later. For now, it's enough to say we live better when we make art. Not only that, we make other people's lives significantly better when we make and share our art. Art heals our bodies, improves our mental health, and creates thriving and connected communities. And yet we are still sold the story that creativity is frivolous, reserved only for children and the retired.

Art is for everyone. I'm not just talking to those of you who want to make art professionally. All art is inherently good. It is inherently responsible. Art creates community, it gives us meaning, it heals us. It is the furthest thing from frivolous that it is possible to be. Which is why we need your art. We need it because it not only helps you but everyone around you.

You have been told that the things you want to create don't matter. We will destroy that lie. If you follow me to the end of this journey, my hope is that you will never doubt your creative calling again. I am here to take you seriously so you can take yourself seriously.

We are storytellers by nature, which means we get to rewrite these stories about what we are meant to be doing with our lives. And we get to put creativity at the centre of them. That doesn't mean it will be easy. We will have to excavate our souls to do so. But the work is exciting, and the reward is worth it: joyful, abundant creation.

'Excavate our souls?' one reader screams. 'But I just wanted to make some art'.

SAME. Unfortunately, the making of things means the making of you. Which is both very annoying and very beautiful. But let me reassure you about a few things. You do not need to have been good at art in school to read this book. You do not need to have taken courses. You don't even need to be a practising artist. But if you are – if you have been in the arts for decades and thrived – you will also benefit from this book. Because this isn't a book about craft. I'm not about to tell you how to use parenthesis to create tension in your novel or how to perfect the scumbling technique with your oil paints. That's a journey for you to traverse through practice, play and mentorship. I am about to tell you how to get out of your own way and recognise that you have art to make. You could research scumbling and parentheses for decades

YOU ARE ALLOWED TO TAKE THIS SERIOUSLY. YOU ARE ALLOWED TO HAVE BIG DREAMS. YOU ARE ALLOWED TO WORK TOWARD YOUR CREATIVE VISION. GO WILD. DARE TO GIVE A F@!#

and never create a thing if you do not also learn to get out of your own way. And we all, wherever we are in the journey, need support as we do that.

This book will start by making a case for creativity. My promise is this: after reading act one of this book, you will know that art, your art, is important, powerful, valuable.

The second act is an anointing, a coronation, a realisation. Together we will realise (or realise again – this process is one of constantly re-realising) that you are an artist, and that your future is going to be full of art. We are going to take the word *artist* off the pedestal and recognise that creativity is yours, now, and is available to you with ease, with joy. Then, through a two-week reset, we are going to create sustainable, unique-to-you creative practices that are resilient in the face of creative blocks. This reset is here to connect or deepen your connection with whatever art is calling your name.

In the third act, we will navigate creative blocks, or what author Steven Pressfield calls resistance. All artists struggle in the process of making art. It is the creative inevitability. In this act, you'll find support as we move through the feelings of shame, avoidance, fraudulence, jealousy and exhaustion.

Then finally, in act four, the largest section of this book, we will explore creative abundance. I want to show artists how abundant and magic their practice can be. Artists should thrive in the process of making art. We will look at how you get good, finish projects, and, if it interests you, chase mastery. We will examine how we develop voice, navigate success, liberate ourselves and celebrate ourselves.

You are an artist and you have so much to give. So this book, in its essence, is a devotion to you. Your ideas, your creativity, your expression. It's here to convince you that you are here to make art, and we absolutely need what you are making. It's here to ensure that you get out of your own way and make the thing. I want this book to envelop you with permission and hope and excitement. You are a onetime phenomenon in the universe, with art to make that has never been made before and will never be made again.

I have sprinkled journalling prompts throughout this book because I want you to consult with you, the artist. You know more than I ever will about your

WOULD IT BE WORTH YOUR TIME, DURING YOUR ONE PRECIOUS LIFE, TO PURSUE YOUR CREATIVE DREAMS?

unique creative journey. I need you to ask yourself questions. To guide yourself. To choose yourself. I want you to become your own muse.

There are no rules on how to answer these prompts. Feel free to write in the margins of this book, think about them in your head, or jot something down in the notes app on your phone. These questions are simply an invitation to realise that you already have the answers, that you are the authority on this creative journey.

I have always learned through journalling. When I read *The Artist's Way* by Julia Cameron in 2017 and started my own journalling practice, it changed my life. I have seen it transform the lives of hundreds of artists. The simple act of looking at your own thoughts is transformative. Research suggests that journalling is a safe and effective way to move through and unblock yourself. I credit the journalling practice with all of my healing and all of my creative success. As long as you're willing to ask yourself questions and notice the repetitive patterns and stories your mind has absorbed, you're doing it right.

It is not easy to undo the stories, to step out of the system, to use your voice and share your art when others won't understand, but we need you. We need your creations, your voice; we need you in your truest expression. It's time to step up. Pluck the strings. Start the painting. Write the book. Do the thing.

It's time to start.

ACT ONE

THE CASE FOR CREATIVITY

Welcome to act one. Here, I will present the case for why creativity is important. I want there to be no doubt in your mind that art has value, that *you* have value as an artist. I want you to see the research. I want you to be armed with the odd fact or figure to pull out when that acquaintance questions your commitment to your craft. I want you to take art seriously, and I want you to take yourself, as an artist, seriously.

Art isn't frivolous, art has value. Art isn't a waste of your time. Making art and sharing it with the world is an act of profound generosity. When you sit down to write, to paint, to make music, you are doing something that is both good for yourself and great for society.

Let us begin.

THE RESPONSIBLE THING TO DO IS TO CHASE YOUR CREATIVE CALLING.

ART: RESPONSIBLE, IMPORTANT, SENSIBLE

Our culture infantilises creativity.

We're told making art is something to be kept in childhood. Something to grow out of. Whether you are creating in your spare time because it brings you joy and purpose or you are trying to go pro, the idea that creativity is 'something for children' pervades our culture.

But this story keeps us small, unfulfilled, purposeless. I grieve the mountains of art left unmade because the creator deemed the project a little juvenile, certainly irresponsible, almost definitely a waste of time.

It is imperative that you understand and deconstruct the narratives that keep artists in creative shame. You can be inundated with craft books and strategies on how to create joyfully and abundantly, but none of these things will stick if you are convinced that your love for creativity is shameful, irresponsible and something not fit for modern society. This chapter is my defence of creativity as one of the most adult things we can do. Making art is the responsible thing, whether you're doing it just for yourself or you're going pro. It is not foolish, embarrassing or indulgent to take creativity seriously.

It's impossible to navigate this idea without first investigating the cultural baggage creative hobbies have that other 'normal' hobbies don't. I want you to meet Jenny (a made-up person, you understand). Jenny plays tennis with her friends several times a week. She does it because it's social and keeps her fit. No one asks Jenny when she's going to finally crack Wimbledon. No one wonders why Jenny is wasting her precious time on the court. Jenny is allowed to play tennis. Because, of course! Why wouldn't she be? Tennis is good. It's EXERCISE. It's SOCIAL. It involves CUTE OUTFITS. I'm not here to argue that people shouldn't be playing tennis. Or going to the gym. Or meditating. Or any other 'acceptable' hobby. I bring up Jenny because I want you to ask yourself why Jenny's hobby is considered legitimate, whereas Esha's isn't.

Esha (also a made-up person but this time an amalgam of the thousands of artists I've worked with over the past decade) writes four times a week for about an hour each time. She's working on a novel. She does it because it delights her, because it gives her a sense of purpose, because it connects her to her inner child, because she just wants to write books! People ask Esha if she's published. If they would have read anything she's written. People say things to her like 'Will you be the next Sally Rooney?' People wonder why Esha is wasting so much time in her fantasyland. She needs to grow up, they say. What is it about Esha's hobby that evokes the ire of otherwise perfectly reasonable partygoers and seemingly well-meaning relatives?

Society has completely missed the mark with creativity. The pervading cultural narrative that art is useless without commerce, comes from people simply not understanding the massive opportunity for self-development that art represents. Creativity is the missing pillar in self-development. Esha's commitment to storytelling is crucial to her well-being, her healing, her sense of self, her life.

But it's not that people are mean or that there's actually anything 'silly' about creating for fun. It's simply that people don't understand. Our culture does not realise the power of creativity. It's not your grandparents' fault that they think writing a book is a waste of time. They simply haven't been told the right story about it.

ARTISTS AREN'T VALUED BY OUR ECONOMY

Gross domestic product (GDP), the magical number economists and politicians spend their whole lives worshipping as if it were a vengeful deity, is, in fact, mostly made-up gibberish. It's meant to be a single number that points to whether an economy has grown or contracted in a period. If people treated it as just one of many guideposts, that would be fine. Unfortunately, it has become something almost mythical, and it's impacting the way society views artists. It now governs a lot of the major conversations about what is and isn't valuable.

With GDP guiding today's prevailing economic thinking, art has very little value. The formulas can't calculate the extra benefit of the delight, meaning and contentment that you, the artist, bring to the world. You and your art have no column in GDP calculations. Just as with other 'unimportant' things like breastfeeding or caring for a sick loved one, the arts are invisible to the economic gods. And that's not even accounting for secondary benefits we'll discuss later (e.g., if you're happier, you make your community better).

In her book *The Value of Everything*, economist Mariana Mazzucato argues that we've lost our way by equating a person's value to society with their income. Despite all the joy and healing art brings, in the eyes of the world, your value as an artist will still come down to your income. In Australia, the arts were hit incredibly hard during the pandemic. But when artists asked for the same relief package from the government as most other industries were given, they were told they were superfluous, undeserving. Why? No one could give a straight answer, but mostly it came down to people with 'real' jobs talking about how they wish they could be paid to sit around and play the piano. As if playing the piano isn't real work or as if it's easy, and artists aren't bringing value to the economy.

Of course, all of us involved in the arts know in our hearts that this is a lie. Yes, we all agree that artists don't make enough money. But we don't agree that that makes us worthless. Our value can be felt everywhere – from the shows we watch, to the music we listen to, to the contentment and joy people feel when they practise art themselves. These things just aren't covered in those abovementioned GDP figures. Imagine if they were! The value of your art cannot be calculated by a simple dollar figure. What you are doing is so much more important than that.

ARTWORK IS REAL WORK.

Indeed, even basic capitalist arguments about the value of the arts aren't true. In their book *Chokepoint Capitalism*, Rebecca Giblin and Cory Doctorow explain how big corporations capture (read: steal) the value artists create. Corporations that have ethically dubious control over large swaths of the creative industries, as both buyers and sellers of creative works set up bottlenecks that allow them to extract maximum value from artists. It's almost impossible for creatives to organise collectively to stop these practices. In other words, creatives generate a lot of money, but the vast majority of it is stolen from them before it hits their pockets.

Artists produce huge amounts of wealth, contributing hundreds of billions of dollars to the economy each year and supporting industries worth hundreds of billions of dollars. But we are constantly gaslit into believing we deserve to be poor because it's in the interest of people in boardrooms who need to hit those quarterly sales figures. Instagram wouldn't exist without creators. Audible, without writers. Sony and Spotify, without musicians. Activision, without coders and game designers. Galleries, without artists. And yet they all subtly and overtly contribute to the lie that there's no money in art. Most of these companies are publicly traded. Go and look at their financials and tell me there isn't anything left for artists. These corporations aren't entitled to a certain amount of profit. They aren't entitled to screw over artists.

The belief that artists don't produce anything 'valuable' doesn't only affect those of you who want to be professional artists. It also affects artists who make art for the joy of it. When we devalue the work of artists, we make all art seem unnecessary and unworthy. Hobbyists and professionals alike grow ashamed of their art. They make less because they internalise stories that tell them they should be doing something 'useful'. We reduce the total amount of art in the world and therefore reduce the total amount of good.

You have value. What you do has value, both in monetary and nonmonetary terms. There are a lot of powerful forces that don't want you to believe that.

You must resist.

CREATIVITY FOR CREATIVITY'S SAKE IS A MODALITY OF SELF-CARE AND SELF-FULFILMENT

No matter what the economists say, no matter what the acquaintances at the party say, we must understand the power of the arts. We invest so much time and money in breath work, exercise, meditation courses, cold plunges, self-help, or whatever other item might be on the checklist this month. But the idea that writing a poem, playing with paints or taking photos could be a part of our routine is dismissed as not proper self-care. Art feels a little too embarrassing. And it's definitely a bit too vulnerable. But vulnerability is *why* it's life-changing. It's this intimacy that makes creativity a practice that will enhance your life.

At the end of an incredible meditation or breath work session, you have had to confront yourself, your mind, your ego. You have witnessed yourself. And it is so beautiful and beneficial. At the end of a creative session, you have also had to confront yourself, your mind, your ego. You have had to witness yourself, and then you *made* something with it. You have a culmination, an alchemy, physical evidence. You have a little bit of you in art form. I'll say it again: creativity is the missing pillar in self-development.

Creation is the opposite of stagnation. It is momentum. It is power. It is agency. And that's the triumph of making art. It's why creativity is worth it even if you aren't Sally Rooney or Florence Pugh or Hans Zimmer. People simply don't realise this. The culture does not give creativity its proper respect as a vehicle for immense personal growth and change. We are told that it is merely a professional exercise. That's why most people don't have anything interesting to say to you at parties. They don't know that when you tell them you write music, you are telling them you are doing intense inner work. They just think you're failing at being a rock star.

This attitude doesn't only make social gatherings a bit uncomfortable, it also ruins your ability to make art consistently and joyfully because it contributes to your creative shame. The person who makes cool shit on the weekends feels immense pressure to legitimise their personal practice by

ARTIST, MAKE SURE YOU CREATE JUST FOR YOURSELF FROM TIME TO TIME.

monetising it. To be clear, I celebrate any creative who wants to sell their art. It's one of the most generous and brave things you can do. And I think you can do it, as we will discuss later in this book. But it must come from the right place. It can't be a means of appeasing capitalistic narratives. It can't be a way for you to seem like a serious person to the rest of the world.

The spectacular irony is that even if you decide to go all in and treat your creativity as a job, the narratives persist. The shame that I felt for taking my writing seriously as an amateur was not solved when I had my first opportunity to try to make writing my full-time job. In fact, it got way, way worse.

In 2018, I was 'gently let go' from my café job, where I wore slippers to work and didn't care whether you ordered skimmed or whole milk. I couldn't pay rent. I moved in with my in-laws. I continued to apply for marketing jobs and admin roles, but essentially, I had the privilege of committing my time to telling stories and writing. For years, all I'd wanted was to make writing my career and now I finally had an opportunity to make a proper run at it. Yet, with all this spare time, I couldn't get through a single day without crying. My word count dropped considerably compared with when I was working at the café. This is no exaggeration. All this free time made for less creativity. When someone asked me what I was doing for work, I wanted to disappear. My inner critic was on a tirade about how foolish and lazy I was to think I could play about for a living. 'Get a real job' was my nonstop mantra. Why was I spending so much time in make-believe worlds (and not even succeeding at that!) when my real adult friends were out there with Excel spreadsheets? I couldn't create because the shame of it was keeping me stagnant.

It wasn't only my inner critic. The 'get a real job' sentiment also came from people I really admired – predominantly other creatives. 'It's just not feasible', 'Only the few make it' and general cynical laughter were some common responses. Some of the feedback came from very successful full-time authors, which was confusing and enraging. Even traditionally successful creatives seemed to have an opinion that this wasn't serious work and that it wasn't a viable or important way to spend my time.

I now think it would have caused less friction to say I was starting a business.

BE WARY OF BETRAYING THE INNER CHILD. YOUR INNER ARTIST, BY TRYING TO BE SOMEONE ELSE'S VERSION OF A RESPONSIBLE ADULT.

I expect feedback would've been different if I'd framed my situation like this: 'I quit my job to start the Executive Prose Writing Corporation. I will be responsible for crafting articulate and engaging narratives that resonate with the target audience, aligning seamlessly with my company's values and goals, and with industry standards'. It wasn't the working-for-myself part that people commented on. It was the art part of what I was doing that seemed dangerous. Art doesn't sell. Art isn't important. Artists make no money. I broke apart when people told me that, and then I would look confusedly around the world I was living in. Art was everywhere, art was what people were clinging to in order to find meaning and joy in their lives. But what I was doing was selfish and silly.

I had a theory about how to solve my shame. Specifically, it was a three-pronged approach to convince the world, and also myself, that art was a reasonable way to spend my time. The three prongs were as follows: (1) get picked by a publisher, (2) get rich off my art, and (3) become famous. How could anyone doubt the legitimacy of a creative life if someone who worked in an office picked me, and then my art made lots of money and got me lots of press?

I see many creatives trapped in this way of thinking. It makes sense; society withholds a sense of legitimacy for amateur, or even working but not yet rich and famous, creatives – so in order to be taken seriously, we need the protection of these three very stable social currencies: corporations, money and fame. But the irony is, it's very hard to find any of these things if your full-time job is being a jerk to yourself about taking art seriously. It's very hard to go pro if you refuse to believe that what you're doing is worthwhile.

That's not the only irony. Because even if you do make lots of lovely money and have lots of lovely fans, lots of lovely people would still much rather you were a lawyer! I would like to take this opportunity to share a text my husband's grandmother sent us on his birthday.

> I hope you and your wife find lots of success, although I cannot understand why anyone would have need of such a service. 😭
> love grandma

ART: RESPONSIBLE, IMPORTANT, SENSIBLE

Grandma knows we now live a beautiful life funded by our creativity. She knows we have an incredible following of artists and that we have a book deal with a major publisher. It still doesn't make sense to her. It's not her fault. We live in a world that cannot understand why creativity is needed.

You can't earn your way out of this creative shame. No amount of money will convince Grandma you're doing a real job. You can't be chosen out of creative shame. No gatekeeper will rescue you from your own preconceived notions that creativity isn't a responsible way of spending your time. And you can't fame your way out of your own limiting beliefs. Impostor syndrome plagues even the most renowned celebrities.

At the same point that I 'went full time' (i.e., full-time crying) with my writing, I started journalling. This, it turned out, was the way I ended up working through my creative shame.

In my journal, I could process the way I saw the world treating the arts. Far worse, I could see the way I was treating my own desire to create. Every day I journalled, and every day I watched myself writing the same things again and again. At first I just witnessed. Then I felt heartbroken. Then I felt rage. Then I began rewriting the narratives. I began calling bullshit.

It was a long transformation over years and years. But then a new voice appeared on the pages of my journal. She understood the power of art, and she was a fierce defender of what I was doing and what I was making. She saved my creative life.

I'm here, writing this book, to make sure you have a voice like that too. Because I believe what we do as creatives, whether we are 'going pro' or creating for ourselves, is one of the most serious and important endeavours we can embark upon as humans.

Society needs more art. It needs to be bursting at the seams with art. Art is one of the most important tools we have for self-development. Art is the culture changer of this world. Art is politically important. Art is the cosy respite for anyone going through pain. Art is a mirror for humanity. It is our place to alchemise trauma into growth, pain into healed wounds, joy into more joy. And even if no one ever sees anything you create, the simple act of regularly

WANTING TO BE A SUCCESSFUL CREATIVE IS NOT CHILDLIKE OR FOOLISH.

IT IS VALID, RESPONSIBLE, AND DOABLE.

making art will make you a fuller version of yourself. In transforming yourself this way, you will be a better friend, spouse, child, parent. When you can unleash your creativity and find a way to discard your stories of shame, you will find that you are not just creating for yourself. You are creating for the world.

So you've been sold a story that art is a little bit frivolous, but nothing could be further from the truth. It is time to let yourself take art seriously. It is time to realise it is not irresponsible or childlike or silly – it is what you are here to do. It is needed. It is responsible. It is generous. It is good.

RESPONSIBLE ART PROMPTS

As we discussed in the introduction, journalling prompts are an opportunity for you to consult with the Creative Authority.

You.

You are the artist. You are the one who has the wisdom and knowledge that will transform your creative life.

A reminder: there is no right way to journal. Consider these questions on paper with pen, on a computer, on your notes app, in the margins. If you are struggling with a question, that is a sign that magic awaits. Push further.

No one else is to read your answers. They are private. They can be messy. Some sentences won't make sense. Good. Let yourself honestly and vulnerably explore these important questions.

Be aware of any resistance and notice what your inner critic says, but keep going. These stories don't go down without a fight. Also, understand that a lot of these limiting beliefs about creativity are there to keep you 'safe'. Making art is vulnerable. We weave a web of stories around our lives to keep ourselves from such vulnerability.

1. **What were you taught about creativity and the arts as you were growing up? What are your inherited stories about artists and artistry?**

Things you might like to look at as you consider this question:

- What do your parental figures think about people who take creativity seriously? Did they take it seriously themselves? Do they consider it to be risky? Are they closeted artists? How did this impact your relationship with creativity?
- What was your experience with creativity in school? Did you have creative subjects available to you? If so, were those who took those classes judged? Respected? Ostracised?
- Were you encouraged to or able to participate in the arts outside of education?
- When you engaged in creativity as a younger artist, what was the response of your kin and friends? For example, if you were in a play, did friends come to watch? Were you supported?
- When you began contemplating careers or post-education work, were there any opportunities or was there any space for you to consider the arts?
- In your current community, do many people have creative hobbies? Are the arts discussed?
- Do you have many people in your life who take the arts seriously or who openly create?

A note: You might have grown up in an encouraging and pro-arts space. I did! That doesn't invalidate any feelings of shame you have around art. I grew up with parents who greatly encouraged creativity, and I went to schools that supported the arts in incredible ways. When I graduated, I was *still* plagued with shame for wanting to take it further.

2. **Write your knee-jerk response to this sentence:** *Art is responsible, important, sensible.* Detail all the resistance that comes up. Let it flow. It's important to understand any biases and narratives you have about creativity. You might notice that some of them reflect and connect with things you detailed in the first prompt.

3. **Vehemently, with vigour, defend your call to the arts.** You can use anything from this chapter to support your defence. It might feel unbelievable, and you might not buy a lot of what you are writing. But I want you to begin rewriting any narratives that belittle or sideline you as an artist.

   Things you might like to write about:

   - Why the arts are crucial to your life.
   - How important your art is and how it is going to impact the world.
   - The benefits creativity gives to your life.
   - A rebuttal to something that was said to you in your journey. Talk back to that time your mother said that your career as a musician would go nowhere. Defend yourself to the friend who laughed at you for your love of watercolours.

CREATIVITY IS THE MISSING PILLAR OF SELF-DEVELOPMENT.

ART HEALS

In this chapter, we are going to look at how art has an impact on us physiologically and neurologically, and consequently how art affects our communities. This is the bedrock, the cornerstone of the case for creativity. It's about how art practically helps you and others. No stone will be left unturned! To make my case for art and its impact on our physical and communal health, I have relied heavily on *Your Brain on Art* by Susan Magsamen and Ivy Ross. This world-changing book looks at the physiological impacts of consuming and making art, and is backed up by an incredible collation of research. The authors' conclusion is profound: art changes communities, our biology, our brains, the world.

I couldn't wait to bring Magsamen and Ross's work into this book, because it grounds the magic of art in science. That inexplicable need to create is actually explicable. *Your art is generous* isn't a wishy-washy lovely sentence.

It's science.

HOW ART CHANGES YOUR BRAIN

Magsamen and Ross explain that art is a vehicle for neuroplasticity. Making art changes the way your brain works because it allows for the creation and strengthening of synaptic connections. Because art provokes multiple intense emotions, it becomes 'salient' in our mind, and salient things have the ability to fire and wire together new neural pathways. The authors look at the responses we have to specific art forms. They note that colours have the capacity to change our respiration, blood pressure, even body temperature. They discuss the FDA-approved music therapy that provides pain relief and increases circulation and mobility. They look at how we physiologically react to poetry and how it helps us to process emotion.

A study by Girija Kaimal from Drexel University found that people who created for as little as forty-five minutes reduced their levels of the stress hormone cortisol. Most importantly, the skill of these artists didn't matter. It was the process of creation, not the product or the outcome itself, that lowered their cortisol.

Similarly, a 2020 study by Senhu Wang, Hei Wan Mak and Daisy Fancourt found that people who participated in the arts more than once a week or who attended cultural events at least once a year had significantly higher life satisfaction. This study was conducted with tens of thousands of people, allowing for variants in lifestyle, economics and geography.

There's also psychiatrist James Gordon, who founded the Center for Mind-Body Medicine. Gordon uses drawing as a tool to manage PTSD symptoms. He concluded that drawing allows a release of 'the fear that has frozen in [the patients'] bodies'. The programs that used drawing as an early intervention for patients who had experienced trauma, reduced symptoms of PTSD by 80 per cent.

Art, whether you are the creator or the consumer, changes you.

Magsamen and Ross write that 'over the last two decades, there have been thousands of studies with outcomes illuminating the reasons diverse art practices, both as the maker and the beholder, improve our psychological state'. If you read their book, you will be inundated with research looking at poetry, dance, painting, quilt work, memoirs and more. There is no art form that is exempt. Least of all yours. Art, your art, is changing you for the better. We need art to be in our arsenal of wellbeing and healing tools. Our brain requires it. The creation and consumption of art belongs next to exercise, meditation, diet, sleep.

HOW ART CHANGES YOUR BODY

I have just scratched the surface of what art does to our minds. But creativity is not a solely cerebral activity. It also affects our bodies.

Art takes care of you on a cellular level. Art actively influences the way your body functions. When art becomes a consistent part of our lives, we are physically healthier. You want some research to back that up? This is now a thriving field of study. How about the experiment where Sean Wu uses music to move heart cells? Or shall we come back to my new favourite person, Daisy Fancourt? In a 2021 study, Fancourt and her colleagues looked at the benefit of leisure activities (art included). They found more than six hundred benefits, including improved respiratory and immune functions. Or maybe we want to look at the study published in *Frontiers in Psychology* in 2021, which looked at the impact of dance on chronic headaches. That study found a statistically significant reduction of pain intensity in the dancers, and sixteen weeks after their dance classes had ended, their chronic pain was still reduced.

Fancourt explains why people are reticent to understand art as medicine. 'People have often viewed the field of arts and health as needing to operate like pharmacology. Whereas, our clear point . . . is that in complexity science, you recognise that there are hundreds of ingredients, hundreds of mechanisms'. Fancourt wants us to understand that while one pharmaceutical drug may have a few specific ingredients that do specific things, art triggers hundreds of reactions in the body. Art is a portal for profound and *varied* healing.

Art affects our bodies. We can use art to heal. We can use art to feel good. To alter our physical experience.

HOW ART HELPS COMMUNITIES THRIVE

In the same vein, your art could be used to support other people's health. Your art can be the tool for other people's healing.

When we think about the art we want to make, a lot of us might begin contemplating how we can serve the market. We might ask ourselves: *What music is consistently hitting the charts? What books are going viral on socials?* But there are other, more exciting questions we might not even realise we can ask. *How could my art support healing sick people? What music supports chronically ill people? How will I serve my patrons' physical and mental health?* You think you are, at best, delighting the world, but you are also healing the world with your art.

Beyond the physiological and mental benefits of art, there are immense social benefits. You won't serve just yourself when you create and share your art, you'll serve the collective. Art heals and enhances communities. Your art will heal and enhance *your* community.

In the aforementioned 2020 longitudinal study, Wang, Mak and Fancourt found there was a distinct but similarly powerful effect that came from regularly attending what the researchers called a 'cultural event', which included things like going to the cinema, seeing an art exhibition or listening to a musical performance. Enjoying art with other people is extremely positive for our mental health. The more art that is available to communities, the better the access to the benefits of art. The more art in the world, the more people are able to experience art's power to heal. When you make art and show it to people, you aren't healing only yourself, you're healing everyone who enjoys your art.

I want to introduce you to Maria Rosario Jackson. Jackson's work focuses on how the arts are a crucial part of healthy communities. In particular, Jackson looks at how marginalised communities have been harmed through the erasure of their culture and arts. It is so easy to think that the only ways to combat large systemic issues like racism and social inequity require hard-nosed, 'practical' solutions like accessible health care and economic support. While that's undoubtedly true, Jackson explains that bringing back art and culture to historically oppressed communities reanchors them to their culture and to each other. Art heals displaced communities. It brings you home to who you are, it allows you to make sense of your situation, and it allows you to reflect on your society and your culture.

We've been told that the arts are an indulgence, but bringing the arts into your community can be life-changing and revolutionary. The arts are an essential form of social activism.

In 2022, the journal *Frontiers in Neuroscience* published a paper called 'More Than Meets the Eye: Art Engages the Social Brain'. The researchers found just that: Art engages the social brain. Art awakens our ability to connect. The researchers saw that 'art engagement recruits the same brain networks as complex social behavior'. Art is made within our societal context; it is a reflection of the community it is born from. Art and human connection share something intrinsic. We've been sold a story that art is a selfish, even isolating activity. But creativity, both the making and consumption of art, is social. It enhances our ability to connect; it is the fibre that knits our communities together.

I live in a really creative village in England. I don't know how I ended up here – I can only assume I was drawn here by some sort of creative magnetism. I didn't know how art filled it would be when I moved to the area. There are world-famous bakers, more than a dozen novelists, incredible muralists and painters, quilters and photographers. Oscar-winning actor Jeremy Irons lives here. Jeremy Irons! Do you know how good it feels to be around so many artists? Do you know how delightful it is to walk down my high street and be bombarded with art? When I potter around my village, I understand why art is so important. Art changes places. Artists change places. There is more and more research to back up this claim, but I don't need the science to feel encapsulated by connection and meaning when I am in creative community. Any time we consume or make art, we feel more connected with each other.

There is much more I could say about the power of art to heal our bodies, minds and communities. What I really want you to take from this section is

WE THINK THAT ART MERELY DECORATES THE WORLD. BUT IT CHANGES IT.

that art has power beyond mere entertainment. This is not a frivolous calling. Art is important for your own health, and for society.

ART HEALS PROMPTS

Our bodies are unique, ever-changing, complex things. Only you can truly understand how your body and your art practice intersect. I leave you with these journalling prompts because you are the authority on this journey. I will keep saying this, but that's because it can take a long time to sink in. You are the artist. You are the authority. You know best.

1. **How does your creative practice affect your body? Do you feel connected to your physical experience as you create? Can you recognise the positive impacts your art has on your body?** There is no correct or good answer to this journalling prompt. Some of us might feel regulated and at peace physically when we create. Others may have no idea how our bodies feel when we create because we are so disconnected from them. For some of us, because of our relationships to ourselves, our bodies and our art, we might feel dysregulated, agitated or distressed. Creative shame can provoke physiological shutdowns as your body desperately tries to protect you from the thing that makes you vulnerable. I once worked with an artist who would come down with the flu whenever they tried to take their art seriously. The body is a powerful thing. We need to start paying attention.

    You may also feel that your body holds you back from your art. Many of us navigate chronic health issues, persistent exhaustion, mental health disorders and disabilities that prevent us from spending time with our art. Acknowledge this, grieve this, process this how you need to. It is all valid.

2. **How do you want your art to influence other people? How do you want it to impact communities? How do you want it to affect other people's**

bodies? Your creations can have an impact on other people's physiology. Let's take that into consideration as we create. As artists, we can be healers. As artists, we can create cohesive and healthy communities. Recognise the power you have. Get clear about how you want to wield it. This should be an exciting prompt. Try to think of all the good you're going to bring to the world.

ACT TWO

YOU ARE THE ARTIST

It is abundantly clear: we need art. In this section, we are going to expand on that statement. We need art, and you're the one who is going to make it. We need art, and you are the artist. We need art, but more specifically, we need YOUR art.

We are about to hold a coronation and anoint you as Artist. We will look at the blocks that are getting in the way of you claiming that title. Then we will examine the act of creation itself. After all, the only way you qualify to be an artist is by making art. We are going to take the creation process off the pedestal and make it doable and reasonable to you. Finally, I will introduce you to the two-week reset – an almost embarrassingly easy fourteen-day program that will render your creative process straightforward and accessible. Whether you've taken years away from your craft or your practice needs a little pep in its step, this program is here to reimmerse you in your creativity.

It's all very well to respect the arts, but it's time to realise that you are the artist and you are the one who is going to make the art.

PICK YOURSELF. SEE YOURSELF. RECOGNISE YOUR MAGIC. BEFORE THEY DO.

CORONATE YOURSELF

You need to give yourself permission to create. You need to anoint yourself as Artist. You need to pick yourself.

What do I mean by pick yourself? We think that being an artist is about external validation, being chosen, being adored, but I have never met a happy artist who hasn't found a way to value themselves and their own work above what the rest of the world thinks. This chapter is about how to make that happen by a process I like to call coronating yourself – putting the crown on your head and saying, 'I choose me before anyone else can. I call myself Artist before anyone has given me permission to do so'. Let's look at all the reasons why it can be so hard to coronate yourself and begin the process of putting on that crown.

WE HAVE BEEN TAUGHT THAT IN ORDER TO CREATE STUFF, WE NEED PERMISSION

Even now, as successful as I've ever been, I can't shake that little voice that tells me I am nothing without external permission, that I need to be picked and chosen to do something as audacious as making things that weren't there before.

This impulse to wait for permission is built into our entire culture. In offices and factories and shops, we nearly always have a superior we defer to for permission. As children we needed parental approval. In our schools we had teachers. So it's not surprising that in our creative life, many of us want someone to tell us that, yes, we are valid, yes, we are allowed. Whether the permission is patronage from the rich, validation from a partner, being offered a contract from a publishing house, or being plucked from obscurity by a casting agent, we consciously or subconsciously believe that if we're meant to do this, someone with authority will let us know.

It also makes sense on a more personal and emotional level that we wait for permission to create because it takes tremendous courage to alchemise parts of our internal world into something external and tangible. Of course we'd feel a little better about making art if someone had told us we were allowed to.

It's hard to pick yourself. It's vulnerable, scary, we haven't been taught how. In fact, we have been actively discouraged by the systems we live in. That's why we have so many artists waiting in the wings, waiting to create but never starting, waiting for life to begin. You need to learn to pick yourself first or else you will always be waiting.

When I tell someone I write books, there's a very high chance that the next question is 'Wow, who publishes you?!' It is nearly always asked with genuine curiosity, but it is hard not to translate 'Who publishes you?' into 'Who gave you permission to do that?'

After years and years of waiting for permission, I picked myself. I published my first two novels by myself. I coronated myself as Author. I looked through my own slush pile and said, *Yes, these books deserve an audience*. I gave myself permission to create, to take this seriously, to take my art seriously. I anointed myself Artist and Author, and it changed my life.

Here are some good indicators that you're waiting for permission:

- You are waiting to create the 'Big Project' until you are more experienced.

- You are waiting to write your book until you have more contacts in the industry.

- You are waiting to share your book until you can find a publisher.

- You are waiting until your children are fully grown to begin. (I see a lot of creatives who don't believe they deserve to create until their kids are older, that their art is selfish. I'd like to counter that nothing is more generous than to prioritise creativity in front of children.)
- You are waiting to start a social media page until you are more experienced.
- You are waiting to call yourself Artist until you are displayed in a gallery.
- You are waiting to call yourself an actor until you have a screen credit (or an Oscar!).
- You create only a few times a month because you tell yourself you'll create more once you're better at it or once you're being paid.
- You're waiting to retire. (Another interesting one. Retirement is seen as a socially acceptable time to return to art. Our society gives the retired permission to be 'unproductive' again.)
- You tell yourself you'll take your art more seriously when you're finally chosen by a gatekeeper.

There are so many ways we withhold permission from ourselves. A lot of the time we do it unconsciously, not even realising we hold the power to pick ourselves. If we've never had that modelled, we've never known it was an option.

But it is. And you must. It may feel deeply uncomfortable, and it will bring to light your limiting beliefs and impostor syndrome, but it will free you of constraints that have kept you small. You will be creatively free.

PICKING YOURSELF ISN'T SOME SECOND-BEST OPTION

Choosing ourselves isn't just something we should do until we 'get noticed'. Rather, it is something we *need* to do every day, until we die. It is the only option if you want to be a joyful, abundant, successful creative.

ARTIST, STOP WAITING TO BE CHOSEN. CHOOSE YOURSELF. TAKE UP SPACE WITHOUT PERMISSION. YOU HAVE TOO MUCH CREATIVE POWER TO BE BEGGING FOR SOMEONE IN A SUIT TO NOTICE YOU.

Consider those who haven't picked themselves but have achieved lots of traditional creative success. You can see the dire consequences for creatives who have received huge amounts of external validation but never validated themselves. They've been given permission by the biggest names in their biz, but they're not having a good time. They aren't joyful. They are creatively blocked or stagnant. They don't like themselves or their art. They feel powerless and exposed to the whims of others.

When this happens, you lose power. Your worth is in the hands of others. You constantly need more and more external validation. You think if you could just get the Oscar, the million followers, the next book deal, then you'd feel good about yourself and your art; then you'd be safe and truly successful. But no matter what you achieve, no matter how many times you are chosen, you never feel like you're enough. Because you're not actually looking for *their* approval, you're looking for your own approval, but you've been rejecting yourself every single day of your creative life.

In my own creative journey, this was a huge realisation. I thought my problem was that agents and publishers were rejecting me. But the issue was that every single day I rejected myself; every single day I begged for other people to back me but refused to back myself. Cultivating the bravery to champion my own art when no one else would has been far more challenging than dealing with rejection from agents and publishers. Rejection really hurts. But it's passive. I don't need to do anything about my ever-growing pile of 'thanks but no' letters.

The action of publicly backing my own writing, however, was active. It required energy, bravery and tenacity. I had to put myself out there. I had to move through vulnerability hangovers from hell. Rewriting the narratives I had about getting permission was some of the biggest, hardest, most profound inner work I've ever done. I thought publishing my own books meant that I had failed. I thought self-publishing was a declaration that no one wanted me. It was a last resort when absolutely everyone had rejected me. It's not true. Coronating myself was strategic. It was a good business decision. It was life-changing. It made me a writer.

HOW TO CORONATE YOURSELF

The easiest, most beautiful way to coronate yourself?

Create.

Sit in the throne of the artist and do what artists do: make stuff.

I think so many of us believe that being an artist comes with a big document of qualifications. You've probably been force-fed narratives that you need to be making a certain amount of money, be working with certain people, be creating for a certain amount of time, have a certain type of body and look a certain way to qualify as a creative person. They're all stories designed to keep you small. These cultural narratives create real systemic and structural issues that negatively affect artists. There are tangible and terrible ramifications. Artists face harmful barriers regarding race, disability, gender and socioeconomic status. Don't gaslight yourself. Discriminatory systems are the gatekeepers of artistry. These issues are real, and you are fighting against institutions and cultures that would rather you be invisible. I see you, I believe you and I believe in your art.

You're not here to lead a small life. You are not here to be unseen or unheard. You are here to take up space and make art.

Making art makes you an artist.

Repeat it. Write it on your walls. Tell people. Sink into this new reality.

Beyond the creative act, you also can pick yourself by sharing your art on your own terms.

Your own terms might mean you share with only a select few, or you never let your family know what you're making. You might choose to never show your face or to use a fake name. You might decide to self-publish. Or to reject the prestigious gallery world of art and make your home a gallery. You may choose to never, ever use a streaming platform and only have your music on vinyl. There are so many 'rules' about how an artist must share their art, but you need to make sure you are giving your creations to the world in a way that feels good.

For me, I held my own coronation on social media. I blocked every single person I knew – Mum, Dad, my partner, everyone from high school – and I positioned myself as Author. I inhabited the role and spoke as Author. I shared my writing. I spoke with authority about the process. In doing this, I created a safe place for me to explore this new identity, away from people who already thought they knew who I was.

Another way to share your art on your own terms is to practise telling people about what you're creating. 'I made this. It delights me. You can ask me about it when we see each other'. You might want to tell only a few people. But telling others about your art is a form of coronating yourself. You are taking up space as an artist.

As I suggested above, you can also share your art without gatekeepers. This looks different within all the various crafts, but you can self-publish, start your own production company, display your art in your own gallery/garden/garage, cast yourself in a film you write and shoot and distribute. None of these options are easy. This work is big, beautiful and challenging. But you're picking yourself when you do this. You're calling yourself worthy.

You can give yourself permission by *literally* giving yourself permission. My method of enacting change is, of course, writing. So, every morning in my journal, I write out permission slips for myself. They look a bit like this:

> I, Amie, give myself permission to publish books on my own terms. I give myself permission to take my books as seriously, or more seriously, than any publisher could. I give myself permission to call myself Author. To speak as someone who knows what she is doing. To show up publicly as an authority in this area and to invest my money in this area of my life.

These permission slips mitigate that feeling of craving permission from someone else. (It also works when I need a rest. Instead of playing linguistic gymnastics with my husband and business partner, James, trying to trick

THIS IS YOUR SIGN TO CHANGE YOUR BIO TO ARTIST/AUTHOR/CREATOR/ACTOR... CLAIM YOUR CREATIVE TITLE. IF YOU ARE DOING THE WORK, MAKING THE MAGIC, THE TITLE IS YOURS. CORONATE YOURSELF. DON'T WAIT FOR PERMISSION.

him into saying something like 'I think you should take the day off today', I just write myself a permission slip.)

The way you give yourself permission will be unique to you. I know creatives who have thrown literal coronations for themselves, with a crown and everything. However you do it, you will need to do it over and over again. You *will* come face-to-face with limiting beliefs about yourself. Stories you've carried from childhood *will* make themselves known. That doesn't mean you've done it wrong. Permission to create art was granted at birth, but that truth has been withheld from you, so it's going to take time to adjust to this new and beautiful reality.

GETTING USED TO THE CROWN

Heavy is the head. The minute you try to take up space and give yourself permission, impostor syndrome will be right there waiting for you. *Who am I to do this? The idea of telling someone that I'm making art is nauseating. What will they think?*

Controversially, I believe that the terrible, achy, whole-body anxiety of impostor syndrome is a good sign. When you've picked yourself and you experience impostor syndrome, it is evidence that you are levelling up. No one who stays safe and small moves through feelings of being a fraud. It is evidence of your bravery. You are growing into new skin. You are becoming something new. You are the pallbearer to the coffin of your old self. When you commit to your art and you feel like an impostor, it is important to know that this means you are doing the work.

That being said, if you let yourself remain convinced that you are a fraud, dressed head to toe in an artist costume, you will burn out. Constantly pretending will drain you. You'll develop a habit of collecting evidence as to why you have no business making art. You make bad art, for starters. You took four weeks off over Christmas. No one knows you make art either. No one buys it. You don't know if you would ever want to sell it . . . no one has told you

IMPOSTOR SYNDROME IS A CLEAR SIGN FROM THE UNIVERSE THAT YOU'VE LEVELLED UP, BABY.

you're any good. You'll lean heavily on thoughts like this, even if you experience huge amounts of traditional 'success'.

In these moments, you need to give yourself profound care. You also need to be strongly reminded that all artists make shit art. That all artists will take time away from their craft. That all artists make mediocre things. That all artists get bored of their own work. Lots of artists don't sell their art. All artists navigate a period when no one tells them they're any good or when their work doesn't sell that well. But that's all for a later chapter.

You are not an exception. You are not special. This is the creative experience. You are living it. The title of Artist is yours. You don't need to wait for permission any longer.

Something else happens when you pick yourself, and this will shock you: you have to make art. This seems obvious, but I think it's a huge reason people are content to wait until retirement, wait until their social media following is bigger, wait wait wait for permission. Because, once you choose yourself, there is work to be done. Scary work. Art work. On the other hand, it feels safe to wait. 'I'm not going to write my magnum opus until I have a bigger audience on social media because what would be the point?' sounds like a very good way of avoiding the vulnerability of actually making something. Waiting for permission is a safety net, a comfortable place to sit without having to face the vulnerability of creation. If you are currently withholding permission, I need you to ask yourself, are you doing it because you're afraid of creating?

Another unexpected but delightful by-product of self-coronation is magnetism. When you pick yourself, people are going to be interested in you. Ironic, no? But it makes sense. If you back yourself, take up space, confidently speak about your art, joyfully create your art, people pay attention. If you want to work with gatekeepers, let them see you working first. Let them see what they are missing. The power you have when they find you doing it yourself, creating on your own terms, without them, is so much greater than emailing them, begging them to pay attention, amidst thousands of others who are asking the same thing. Choosing yourself turns the tables. It transforms the power dynamics that have been prevalent between artists and gatekeepers for a long, long time. It is revolutionary.

This magnetism goes well beyond wooing gatekeepers; it attracts all sorts of synchronicities and little miracles. The conversations you have become far more interesting. You begin, whether you realise it or not, to give permission to others to follow in your footsteps, and opportunities to collaborate and create start popping up without you even trying that hard. You are no longer looking outside of yourself; all the power comes from within.

Choosing yourself doesn't mean you don't doubt yourself or you never feel the pain of rejection. It isn't a cure-all for creative pain. It is a choice we make each day, each moment. It is incredibly challenging, and I need you to do it.

Before we finish this chapter, I want to pick you. I know, I know, I said that you can't wait for permission from anyone but yourself. And I was right. This coronation I am about to hold for you won't mean shit compared with the one you hold for yourself. But I'm still going to do it. You deserve to hear these words.

You are here to make things.

You are qualified simply because you were born.

Your curiosity about creativity is qualification enough.

This is your purpose.

You can prioritise art.

You are doing what you are meant to do. Even in your mess, even in your inconsistency, even in your learning phases, you are Artist. Creative. Maker.

CORONATION PROMPTS

Coronation time. It is time to choose yourself on the pages of your journal, in the notes app of your phone, in the margins of these pages. This is holy work.

ARTIST, WHEN YOU TAKE UP SPACE WITHOUT PERMISSION, YOU BECOME MAGNETIC.

1. **What actions am I not taking because I have not been given permission?**

    Further questions to consider as you answer the prompt:

    - What am I 'saving' to create until I am chosen?
    - What am I refusing to feel before I am chosen?
    - Are there certain milestones I am waiting for before I am allowed to create or share certain things?

    You might like to investigate how it feels to come face-to-face with some of these realisations. But be very gentle on yourself. We have been taught to wait. Taught to seek permission. It is within our culture to stay small until told otherwise.

2. **What permission slip do you need right now? How can you self-anoint? Self-coronate?** This prompt may feel rebellious and maybe even ridiculous. Push into those feelings. You should feel audacious. Use your answers from prompt #1 to aid you in answering this question. You can even word it like an actual permission slip, like the one I showed you earlier in this chapter.

SMALL MAGIC

The most convincing, regal and holy coronation you will hold is the one that happens every single time you make art. Every time you sit down to create, you are calling yourself an artist and then following up that proclamation with an action to prove it. In this chapter, we are going to make sure you are not just an artist by name. We are going to make art easier. Approachable. Doable.

I romanticise nearly everything in my life, from the cup of coffee I cradle in the mornings to the barefoot walks I take in the countryside. It's rare you'll find me without my rose-tinted glasses. I see magic everywhere and believe everything has a glimmer of the divine. But when it comes to the creative process, I have become uncharacteristically pragmatic.

ART IS IMPORTANT. ART IS GOOD. BUT ART IS NOT A BIG ACT OF GOD. IT IS NOT A MIRACLE.

Rather, it is a million tiny mundane miracles, performed not by the muses but by you.

I have found that creatives, bless us, want fantasy in everything, and never more so than in the process of making things. There is nothing more god-like, more wizard-like, more fantastical than the spontaneous upwelling of creativity. But when I create, I slip my rose-tinted, half-moon spectacles down my nose and allow myself to look at this logically. I allow myself to take this seriously. I become workmanlike. I write my five hundred words each weekday. I wait for no muse. I am the muse. I do not need the perfect setting. I am the artist, therefore, I make art. And bizarrely, when I take this approach, this is when I have the most fun, this is when I become my most creative.

Creatives excuse their blocks by blaming the muse. We set standards for our art that keep us feeling perpetually incapable. Yes, it would be lovely if we could hold a sort of séance for the muses, involving chanting and candles and a big gulp of good red wine. It would give us a ton of dopamine if we then set aside a day to write ten thousand words (polished words, mind you, no crap here!), and if our children didn't exist in the times we were in the studio, and if the studio were a greenhouse in Austria with the constant smell of early spring jasmine where the light is only ever golden hour. Then, finally, maybe, we could actually produce something! This is how many of us think creativity should feel: a collection of perfect circumstances that calls forth a divine power.

But this attitude does not free you to delight in creative abundance. It hampers you.

For a long time, I used to demand a lot from my creative practice. I felt that if I dared to be someone who made things, I better be the most productive creative the world has ever seen. If I dared to take myself seriously, then my word count should be pretty serious. I believed that I needed an entirely free day to write, and I would try so hard to cultivate it. To cancel everything. Wipe the board. Clear the decks. And then, when once in a blue moon I would manage it, I would spend the whole day crying. It was too much pressure. The day was too empty. I felt overwhelmed with the desperation to make as much as possible within the time I had to spare. *I should be able to write at least three thousand words today,* I would think. On those days, I would be very lucky if I managed more than two hundred.

This isn't just a me problem. It is a familiar story for many of the creatives I work with. They tell me, 'I want to write three thousand words a day! I want

THERE ARE NO BIG STEPS TO TAKE, ONLY BABY STEPS.

to write an album in a week! I want to spend ten hours painting on my day off!'

Our obsession with big creative goals is one of the major reasons people can't make art. It is perfectionism and self-sabotage dressed up as ambition and enthusiasm. You tell yourself, *If I'm going to spend time creating, it better be the most productive time in my life.* The hustle of it soothes the narrative that art is a waste of time. *If I make it a grind, if I make it into a game of productivity, it makes the fact that it's an art project a little less embarrassing.*

We are no longer a society interested in good-quality work and actual results. We are a society concerned with conspicuous busyness and perceived effort. We are living in a culture that cares more about how hard it looks like you're working than what you're actually making. High-quality creative work does not need to come from an endless grind. Forget how hard it looks like you're working: I just want you to make art. Who cares if you spend all of January lounging around, not creating, then for the rest of the year you compose and produce your next EP?

Big goals give us HUGE dopamine hits and feel really good in the moment but they aren't how we make wonderful art. We create best through small, consistent steps performed regularly. If you look into the routine of most successful creatives, you'll find that hardly any of them devote entire days to creativity. In his book *Deep Work*, Cal Newport argues that top performers tend to be people who can find just a few hours a day working in a high-quality, focused way. And that's professionals at the top of their field! Here most of us are, people with full-time jobs, families, bodies to look after, and we're trying for double or triple what full-time, highly experienced artists are doing.

I want you to take a step back and set goals that are reasonable and doable. Small goals. Bare minimums. Minimum viable progress, as Greg McKeown, author of *Essentialism*, would say. For example, you spend time with your guitar for fifteen minutes before bed. You draw one tiny, stamp-size doodle per day. Every Wednesday and Friday you record a monologue.

Taking small, consistent steps is the journey to creative mastery.

Small, achievable goals will protect you from burnout, help you stay in contact with your identity as an artist long-term, produce better quality AND quantity in the long run, and generally just feel better. There is no WRITE A BOOK. There is only write one hundred words. There is no PAINT A MASTERPIECE. There is only fifteen minutes with the brushes, stroke by stroke. There is no COMPOSE A SOUNDTRACK this coming Tuesday. There is only working on a few lines of your composition every Tuesday so you can be done within the year.

A writer wants to write a book. They get a blank whiteboard out and write in big block letters, WRITE BOOK. This feels really good. They get a dopamine rush. Their first writing session actually goes really well! They write twenty-five hundred words. Amazing. If a book is about eighty thousand words, they'll get there in only thirty-two days of writing! In theory, that's true. But in practice, something else happens. The next day, they go to write and that initial rush is gone. They don't have any good ideas. Instagram is right there. They have one hundred unread emails in their inbox, each offering the promise of progress. Even the vacuum cleaner starts to look like fun. They know they have to write twenty-five hundred words today, and yet they can't even write one.

They stare at a blank page and end up writing nothing. A month goes by like this, maybe two. Then they get another huge burst of inspiration. Yes! Things are looking up. They write another twenty-five hundred words on some random Tuesday. Now, in two months, they've written five thousand words. But they also don't really feel like a writer, and that goal of eighty thousand words suddenly doesn't feel like it's thirty-two days away, it's actually thirty-two *months* away working like this.

Compare this with the writer who has set themselves a baby goal of three hundred words a day, five days per week. They don't need to have huge amounts of motivation to complete this goal. It seems really doable each time they sit down to write. As a result, they don't suffer from that mix of fear and panic that so often leads to writer's block. They start to chain together writing days. Over time, writing feels like a core part of their identity. They grow in confidence, and, despite their smaller word goal, it's taken them only about eight months to finish their whole first draft. They come out of the process much less stressed, much more in touch with their inner creative, and loving the process.

Which writer would you rather be? I see the first story so often. I saw it first in myself, during the first six years of trying to finish a book. It is one of the biggest mistakes creatives make.

I want everyone to finish this book understanding that you can create abundantly without working yourself to the bone, without big promises, without burnout.

SMALL GOALS BUILD YOUR IDENTITY AS AN ARTIST

Small goals mean you're both more rested and more creative. Small goals are a way to rebel against a culture that is obsessed with hustle. Small goals allow you to creatively thrive.

It is time to put your ego to the side and make some embarrassingly small creative goals. It's time to take the creative process off the pedestal. Take art seriously, but don't idolise it. You're made to create. This process doesn't need to be hard. It's just art. It's what you're made to do.

Please romanticise your life, Artist. Please decorate your days with little miracles and indulge in all the idyllic, fairy-tale magic you can. Please invite romance into your art, write the idealistic love story, paint like the Pre-Raphaelites, design clothes that have no real business being worn day-to-day, but do not be idealistic about your creative practice. Do not put artistry on a pedestal. Do not sacrifice yourself to the narratives that you must go big or go home. Art is human, messy, imperfect, and that is exactly as it should be.

SMALL MAGIC PROMPTS

In the next chapter we will look at making small creative goals, so for now I just want you to gently investigate some of the ways you might have put art on a pedestal.

1. **In what ways have you put art and your creative process on a pedestal?** The strange thing about going on your creative journey is that you are simultaneously fed stories about how artists are losers while also being told that artists are untouchable elites. We've already looked at some of our inherited beliefs about why art is foolish and shameful, but now, ironically, we must look at how we've been taught to put artists on a pedestal.

   Things you might like to consider as you write about this:

   - What rules do you have around your creative process? For example, do you have to create in certain conditions? Do you have to get a certain amount done in order to feel like it was a 'good session'?
   - When you look at your creative heroes, what do you believe makes them successful? Do you have stories about why they are such good creatives?
   - Do you believe you have to have certain qualities in order to be a 'good artist'? What are they?
   - Do you find yourself waiting for inspiration?
   - Do you believe that creatives have to come from a certain background? Have a certain education? Detail these beliefs.

2. **How is your creative process influenced by the answers from the previous prompt?** I want you to consider how the romanticisation of the artistic process and the idolisation of the artist has affected your own

journey as a creative person. For instance, you may believe that art should be guided by the muses and you should create only when inspired. The consequence: it takes a very, very long time to complete projects. You also might feel your creative process benefits from your answers (e.g., I say a creation prayer to the gods before I create, and it always puts me in the right headspace to create).

IF YOU CHOOSE TO BE AN ARTIST, YOUR LIFE WILL LOOK DIFFERENT FROM EVERYONE ELSE'S. AND THAT IS HARD. AND IT IS ALSO REALLY BEAUTIFUL.

THE TWO-WEEK RESET CHALLENGE

You are an artist. Even when you've spent a long time away from your art, you are still an artist. But nothing reaffirms our identity as a creator like creating. The purpose of the next challenge is to bring you back to the art. So, before we continue with the book and really get to work on your creative blocks, I want you to do something. I want you to make art. 'What?' you ask. 'Aren't I supposed to make art only once I've resolved all my blocks?' I'm so sorry, but no. For you to get to the most out of this book, I want you to get into the habit of creating, blocks or no. The intention of this chapter is to make that as easy as possible for you.

In the following pages, you'll find a program that doesn't ask much of you, that is achievable, that doesn't require perfection or anything close to it, and that gets results. And this works for all creatives at all stages. This challenge is:

- Great for creatives who have fallen out of step with their creative practice and want support as they reengage.
- Here to support creatives who want to show up more consistently and in the spirit of small magic.
- Here to support creatives who have been stuck in the planning/preparing/researching stage and need a kick in the creative behind to actually get making.

- Here for anyone who struggles with perfectionism around how and when to show up to create.
- Here for those creatives who are stuck in patterns of procrastination and avoidance.
- Particularly good if you're experiencing any sort of resistance to create at all.

Use this program again and again if you ever get stuck in your journey, if you're in a slump and need a reset, or if you've been away from your art for a while. While you go through it, I want you to pay attention to all the little stories that come into your head: the resistance, the fear and also the joy!

Okay, let's get started.

THE PROGRAM

I call this program the two-week reset. It is here for you whenever you need to come back to the basics of what it is to be an artist. Been on holiday and want to get back into a routine? Two-week reset. Gone through an entire year of procrastination? Two-week reset. Got a new project that you're excited to dive into, but not sure where to start? Two-week reset. It's here to support you whenever you feel like you've wandered off the creative path. It's a reboot and a reignition of all your creative ways.

STEP ONE: PICK A SMALL CREATIVE GOAL

Choose a bare minimum amount of time (e.g., ten minutes of piano) or a bare minimum amount of creative output (e.g., a hundred words).

Whatever you came up with, I'm going to stop you right there and ask you to *at least* halve it. We want this goal to feel so beautifully doable, it would almost be embarrassing to tell someone about it.

CONSISTENCY AND SELF-COMPASSION ARE THE ANTIDOTE TO MISTRUSTING YOURSELF.

For example, instead of planning to write two thousand to four thousand words a day, plan for two hundred to four hundred. Instead of planning to paint anywhere from three hours a day to a full day, try ten to twenty minutes a day. Instead of editing an entire YouTube video in a day, just work on a minute or two of footage.

Once you reach your maximum number, you're done. You have to stop. Even if you want to keep going, you have to stop. Please. This is about completing the challenge and building up that belief in your ability to show up consistently. It's not about burning yourself out in one blaze of glory. I would actually prefer it if you stopped when you hit your minimum. I put the maximum in there because I know some of you need to be told there's an upper limit. The minimum is actually the thing to strive for. The minimum should reflect what you can do with basically no effort. It should show you that creativity doesn't have to be scary or exhausting and that you are capable of following through on promises you make to yourself.

I know it's going to feel underwhelming but trust me when I say this process is life changing. When you trust yourself to show up, art gets made. Shitty art, mediocre art, world-changing art – you'll make all of it at some point if you trust that you will show up when you want to show up.

STEP TWO: PICK ONE TO THREE CONSTRAINTS

The idea here is to further limit the amount of work you can possibly do. To narrow your options. The fear of the blank page is often a fear of choice. By picking some deliberate constraints, you will limit the amount of fear too.

Some possible constraints to consider:

- The screenwriter is not allowed to reread a scene or have more than two characters on-screen at any time.
- The poet can only use up to twelve syllables per line and eight lines for the whole poem.

- The novelist isn't allowed to research during drafting and can only describe physical spaces through dialogue.
- The painter can only use the colours black and red, and will keep going on the same artwork until it satisfies the 80 per cent rule (see the perfectionism chapter).
- The illustrator is not allowed to start over once they've made the first mark.
- The BookTuber can only make a review that is five minutes long, is done in a single take and is unedited.
- The actor can only practise monologues shorter than three minutes.
- The jeweller can only use a single metal in their next piece.
- The potter can only make plates.

As a general rule, constraints should always *reduce* your perfectionist tendencies. They should be there to make it less likely you'll freak out about the quality of your work and just let you *do*.

STEP THREE: PICK A TIME

The benefit of working toward a small goal is that you should be able to fit your creativity into a similarly small block of time.

You can start with setting aside the same time each day. I have found this regular schedule helps. I've written most of my novels between 8:00 and 9:00 a.m. My body is used to writing then. It expects it. That's powerful. It also takes away potential decision fatigue because you know when you have to show up. When you've picked a specific time, take your phone and set a recurring alarm that goes off at that time. Protect that time. When people want to take your creating time away from you, show them the alarm.

However, if you're the type of person who might encounter something else infringing upon this time, thus making you give it up completely, consider setting a more general time, like 'after the kids are in bed' or 'once I've finished regular work for the day' or 'after I brush my teeth in the morning but before I leave for work'. These are harder to set an alarm for, but you can leave a note on your bathroom mirror to remind you that when you're done brushing, it's time to start strumming. Or maybe your phone background asks the questions, *Are the kids in bed? Could you be creating?* Make it as easy as possible for yourself.

STEP FOUR: SET UP YOUR SPACE

Environment is important, but obsessing over it can also get in your way. I want you to give yourself five minutes maximum to make your environment as conducive to art as possible. Put a timer on. I recommend setting your phone to airplane mode, putting on some music and decluttering. Have all your equipment ready too. When that timer goes off, you start creating. No more fussing with your space.

STEP FIVE: DO THIS EVERY DAY FOR TWO WEEKS

This is the simplest step to explain but the hardest to stick to. But hopefully you've picked a goal that is so simple you can do it when you're half-asleep, or crazy busy, or feeling entirely uninspired.

If you can't or don't think you can meet your goal every day, I want you to go back and halve it again. Make it so that the worst version of yourself will stick to this program for two weeks. Even then, as I'll talk about later, you might not hit every day. And that's okay. It's sort of the point, in fact.

COMMON QUESTIONS

There will be resistance. When we do scary things – and art is nearly always a little bit scary – we resist. Following are some of the most common resistances to the two-week reset challenge.

YOU ARE ALLOWED TO ENJOY YOUR CREATIVE PROCESS. ART IS ALLOWED TO BE EASY!

ALL I'LL MAKE IS A FEW LITTLE PIECES OF ART. IS IT WORTH IT?

You might think, *Is that it? All I'll produce are few little pieces of art?* I refer you back to the 'Small Magic' chapter.

Remember: Art can be really simple. Art can be easy! Show up a little bit, regularly. That's the magic of the two-week reset. You don't need to make any big gestures. Relieve yourself of the pressure of being the most productive artist of your generation. Embrace your identity as someone who makes a little bit of progress every day. I promise you, something magic is about to happen when you touch base with your art every day.

WHAT HAPPENS IF I MAKE REALLY BAD ART?

I really, really hope you do. Bad art is a non-negotiable part of an abundant creative practice. Bad art is the stepping stone to mediocre art, which is a stepping stone to the mastery of art. You must allow yourself to make some crap over the next two weeks. These next fourteen days are actually a delightful, creative, outright war on your perfectionism. We will go over shitty art in more detail later in the book. Suffice to say, once you embrace letting yourself just create without worrying about the quality, true magic happens.

Too many of us have been taught that not excelling is dangerous. But it is safe to make bad art. You are safe as you play those 'terrible' tunes, write those cliché sentences or film that embarrassing self-tape. More than that, you are thriving, playing, delighting.

That being said, your inner critic may have a bit of a feeding frenzy over the next fourteen days, so when it begins spewing bullshit, pick a few of these helpful phrases. Keep them close, have them as your phone background, on a sticky note or written on your hand.

- You're thinking these things because you are frightened, and it's okay to be scared.
- You are doing so much better than you realise.

- Shitty art is the stepping stone to the mastery of art.
- This is not the final version.
- You've been taught that creativity isn't safe, but we are taking deep breaths, safe at home, completely and utterly protected.
- What we are doing, however little, is a generous act.
- You are allowed to be upset; we are going to try again tomorrow.
- I am so unbelievably proud of you.
- This is the start of magic.
- I am incredibly special.
- Art is allowed to be easy.
- Art is allowed to be hard.

WHAT HAPPENS WHEN I SCREW UP? HAVE I FAILED?

It's likely you will screw up, and yes, this means you failed.

But I hope you screw up. I hope you miss a day.

So many creatives are so frightened of their inner critic, of the language they would use if they fail, of the stories they'd engage in upon encountering failure, that it can feel safer just to opt out of art completely. You may be familiar with this line of thinking: 'I've failed now, so I give up'.

But failure doesn't mean self-betrayal. Failure isn't a full stop. In fact, this is an incredibly important part of the two-week reset challenge. How will you treat yourself when you miss a day, or two? Your response is just as important as the showing up itself.

My preference is that you do screw up somewhere in these two weeks. This program is here to do more than build and recover your ability to trust in yourself. It is also here to address the 'Oh, I've screwed it up, so what's the point in continuing?' narrative. Failing and then having the courage to try again the next day is one of the most important skills we have as humans. Let's build it. Let's learn how to navigate failure.

So what do you say to yourself if you skip a day? What's going to happen if you 'mess up' on the promises you intended to keep?

I want you to prepare an 'I screwed up' message for yourself for these days when you fail. Do it now, before something goes amiss. We are preparing to fail because failure is a normal and expected part of this journey.

Let me give you an example:

> Screwing up doesn't mean you're a screwup. Success and fulfilment don't come without blips and errors along the way. This is a holy and important part of my journey. This isn't a sign to give up. It is a sign to carry on. I have so much to give, and I refuse to let these moments get between me and my art. I am allowed to be disappointed, but I do not allow myself to stop. I hereby recommit to my [insert your BABY goal] – and I cannot wait to prove to myself that failure isn't a full stop. I am doing so much better than I realise.

Please feel free to use my message or parts of it. A lot of us don't have a compassionate inner voice yet because we've spent our entire lives being our own worst enemies.

This might be the point where you think, *If I am this nice to myself and let myself get away with failure, I'll just keep failing because there are no consequences for not following through.*

First of all, there are always consequences for not following through: art doesn't get made.

Second of all, there is absolutely no evidence that negative reinforcement improves performance. In fact, research says otherwise. There are multiple studies that look at how positive reinforcement creates lower stress, and more success.

Your inner critic isn't holding you together. It isn't keeping you in line. It is

ARTIST, YOU DON'T GET TO AVOID FAILURE.

keeping you in a state of high stress, and with a much higher likelihood of failing. It is holding you back from creative abundance.

We have been taught by school, work and society in general that when we fail, we deserve some sort of punishment. It makes sense that we would beat ourselves up and emotionally punish ourselves when we screw up. But this narrative is just that, a narrative.

A new narrative I would like to engage in is this: The anger you harbour against yourself is learned and undeserved. When you fail, you need compassion. You deserve compassion.

WHAT HAPPENS AT THE END OF THE TWO WEEKS?

At the end of the two weeks, even if you screwed up a few times, you'll have proven to yourself that you can imperfectly but loyally show up for yourself.

You said you would do something, and you did. I am so proud of you.

You might've screwed up, but you got back to it. I am so proud of you.

This is the foundation of a creatively abundant life.

WHAT DO I DO NEXT?

Let me start by telling you what you are absolutely not going to do:

You are not going to decide to significantly up the goal for your regular, non-challenge creative practice.

Don't.

It's self-sabotage. Even if you don't fully understand it in that way. You are still learning to trust yourself. Instead, keep going with small, achievable goals. I want you to truly understand how small things make big things.

Please consider this list of things you might want to do instead:

- Celebrate! You deserve to celebrate; you've spent the last two weeks proving to yourself that you can follow through on your own word. Do something that delights you. Know that I am celebrating with you.

- Lower your goal. Now that you're not officially doing the challenge, you might want to make it even easier for yourself to keep up a consistent practice by going for a lower goal.

- Start the challenge again. There is no limit to how many weeks you can keep doing this! It's here for you if you ever feel stuck, defeated, like a fraud, or like you're losing trust in yourself. Most artists fall off the wagon. Most artists go through slumps. We face rejection, burnout, procrastination, ridicule and the constant misunderstanding of friends, relatives and strangers. It's normal that you might need to take a step back and begin again.

Whatever you choose to do after your fourteen days of small magic, I want you to know that this challenge is here for you whenever you need it. It can become the foundation of your creative practice. It can form the base of the way you show up for your creativity – not with big gestures but with small, divine and holy promises. It can become a daily habit that grows into an amazing project, career, life.

Your practice doesn't have to be intimidating and overwhelming. Your creative journey can be filled with ease and flow. I want you to know that I have built my entire career on small goals like this. It works. You can do it the easy way.

ACT THREE

BLOCKS

So many artists think that being blocked is a sign that they aren't ready, that they aren't good enough, that they should quit. But resistance is a signpost toward mastery, growth and change. When you meet with a creative block in your journey, you are feeling the tension between where you are right now and who you are becoming. As Steven Pressfield has taught us, resistance is an invitation to your own creative evolution.

When you create, there is no hiding from yourself. In that way, making art reminds me of journalling. You confront your ego, your thoughts, your past. Creativity is a process of knowing yourself. Art reveals all. Which is why so many of us avoid art. We would rather not be confronted with all that darkness. But creativity will also reveal the light within you. It will reveal the treasures within you and demand that you express your potential. In other words, the creative process is very much worth it, despite the discomfort of feeling blocked or stuck.

In this section, we will navigate the most prominent creative blocks: procrastination, perfectionism, jealousy, comparison and burnout. There are many types of creative blocks, but this lot are the horsemen of the creative apocalypse. Despite that dramatic comparison, I want you to know that they are not your demise. You will not be able to avoid any of these creative blocks, but you will be able to navigate them safely, and they're going to teach you a lot about yourself along the way.

RESISTANCE IS THE SIGN THAT **MAGIC AWAITS YOU.**

ON PROCRASTINATION

Before we start this conversation, I'm going to invite you to clean the whole house, wash the dishes and take the dog for a second walk. No, wait, excuse me – I'm going to invite you to sit down right here, right now, and read a chapter about procrastination.

No matter how many times you do the two-week reset challenge, no matter how many productivity apps you get on your phone, even if you become James Clear himself and atomic all your habits, you will procrastinate. You will run in the opposite direction of your art on many occasions. You will hide from your art. You will stop creating. All of this is a part of the creative journey.

This chapter will not be about eliminating distraction. It won't be filled with hacks and tips to elevate your productivity. I will not be recommending apps. Instead, this chapter will be about your lifelong relationship to your art and how we can create a sustainable, delightful, consistent practice while having a manageable and healthy relationship with procrastination. I want you to know what to do when you come face-to-face with the desire to run. I want you to know how to care for yourself on month three of avoiding your art. I want you to be prepared.

PROCRASTINATION HAS EXISTED FOREVER

Before we go any further, you must understand procrastination is not a modern blight.

'But social media! The internet!' Or maybe, if you're reading this in the twenty-second century, it will be fully immersive VR blockchain android hyper-sims. 'It has poisoned this generation of creatives!' Distraction and the artist have had a millennia-long love affair, one that's simply changed shape with the centuries. Victor Hugo wrote naked to ensure he didn't distract himself by going outside when he worked.

Social media is OUR distraction, and yes, there are very clever people who make apps that are some of the most addictive distractions ever seen, but it is distraction itself and procrastination itself that must be addressed. Examining the reasons we turn away from our art is a far more fruitful journey than just deleting all the apps (although that also helps sometimes). Trust me, if you do delete everything, you *will* find something else to procrastinate with. What I want you to understand is that whatever distracting concoction someone has come up with in a fluorescent-light-filled Palo Alto mega-office has absolutely nothing on the joy, wonder and meaning that creativity can bring. If you can find intrinsic motivation, if you can hook into what you love about the creative process, tech bros cannot hijack your mind. That's not to say you will never procrastinate again. You will, however, find that it becomes a much smaller problem in your life. How? We'll get to that later. Once we can understand that we are not specifically or exceptionally doomed, we can move on to building a relationship with procrastination that is healthy.

Yes, you have some super potent distractions.

But no, you aren't screwed.

WITNESSING YOUR PROCRASTINATION

Witnessing your avoidance and understanding your patterns of procrastination are both crucial to a long and abundant creative practice. Let's say you're a week into the two-week reset. You've been consistently showing up in small ways, making shitty art. But this week has turned south. You showed up only once, and you didn't reach the bare minimum. There was too much going on. And you weren't really sure what to do next in the project. Now you're out of the routine, and you're thinking, *I've screwed up, I might as well give up.*

During these moments when you feel like you've failed, please know, I'm excited for you. *This* is the moment where you get to do the *work*. In the moment when you don't want to return to the art, when you're looking anywhere but to the art itself, you get to witness procrastination. Look it in the eye and begin to understand it.

I don't want you to eliminate avoidance. I want you to look at what's happening. When creatives come head-to-head with procrastination, we see it as an external problem to be solved. We buy apps, we read books, we have strategies. It's an emergency. We must fix it. The tips-and-tricks approach to procrastination may get you somewhere, but it will not buy you a long and abundant creative life. I am not asking you to solve procrastination. I am asking you to understand it.

INTERPRETING YOUR PROCRASTINATION

Too often, we witness our procrastination and then misinterpret what we are seeing. We avoid the art and then start asking all the wrong questions: Am I lazy? What is wrong with me? Am I not meant to be an artist? We translate avoidance of the art as a sign that we are not enough. This is a mistranslation that ruins lives and robs the world of art. Procrastination means nothing of the sort. Procrastination is simply evidence that we are, in some way, afraid. Instead of asking yourself whether you are enough or have what it takes, you need to ask yourself questions that uncover what is actually happening for you as you avoid the art. My favourite question to ask myself when I am avoiding my art is this: What am I running from?

I've been procrastinating writing this paragraph and so I'll use myself as

WITNESS YOURSELF AS YOU LEAVE YOUR ART MIDSENTENCE, MIDSTRUM, MIDSTROKE. ASK YOURSELF, WHAT AM I RUNNING FROM?

an example. What am I running from? The answer: I'm running from the feeling of being stuck. I am running from the discomfort of looking at writing that doesn't feel good enough yet. Whenever I return to this paragraph I get that horrible feeling of 'I don't know what to do'. And that feeling is uncomfortable and scary. Now that I understand why I keep picking up my phone every time I return to this section, I can take care of myself accordingly. I don't need a barrage of guilt and shame for struggling to pay attention, I don't need to be 'more disciplined' or to 'try harder'... I need to remind myself that even when I am not sure what I am writing, with time, I always figure it out. I don't need to give up being an author; I need to remember that shitty art is mandatory in this process of making art. This paragraph is allowed to be shitty, for now. I need to remember that I won't immediately have the answer to all my creative problems, but the answer, in one form or another, comes. I tell myself to be patient, and as I do, I feel my body relax. My resistance lessens. I type.

When you avoid the art, ask yourself, *What am I running from?* Check in with your body. What's happening physiologically? Are you in flight mode? Why? Procrastination holds the keys to some of our most monstrous blocks, if we only dare to determine why we are running away.

WHEN PROCRASTINATION IS PROBLEMATIC

Procrastination is not always a problem. There's a fascinating 2021 study by Jihae Shin and Adam Grant that suggests that, in fact, the most creative people are usually mild procrastinators. That is, they dillydally over tasks or maybe wait to feel a bit of urgency before they begin something. That's all completely normal. Taking longer than you'd like to finish something isn't criminal. Your pace of creating will be entirely unique to you, and whatever that pace is, whether it's incredibly fast or slow, stuttering and starting; it is holy. In fact, according to Shin and Grant's study, it seems people who procrastinate a little might have more ideas than people who don't procrastinate at all. The problem comes when you start putting things

WE DON'T PROCRASTINATE BECAUSE WE ARE LAZY.
WE PROCRASTINATE BECAUSE WE ARE SCARED.

off for weeks, months or years. When procrastination becomes chronic, it can destroy you.

Chronic procrastination fractures your relationship with yourself. We touched on this in the two-week reset, and it's a major reason I wanted you to spend time building up that trust in yourself. I've witnessed procrastination worm its way into artists' lives, then grow into mouldy, deep self-loathing. If you leave procrastination unchecked, it can be an incredibly dangerous and debilitating form of self-sabotage.

When you promise to make and create, and then you fail to follow through, it's upsetting. When you promise to chase the thing your heart calls for thousands of times over and you never show up for yourself, it ruins your relationship with yourself.

If somebody else were treating you this way, you would've gotten rid of them years ago. If you hired someone to do a job and they repeatedly refused to turn up, you would fire them, probably after the first week. If they showed up but they were on their phone the entire time, they'd maybe last a few weeks. If you had a friend or a partner who repeatedly bailed on you, put someone else before you or betrayed you, you wouldn't or shouldn't maintain that relationship. It's a crap relationship and you deserve more.

When you ask yourself to write for ninety days straight and never show up, even though it's something you really want to do, you are screwing yourself over and doing damage to the way you relate to yourself.

Over time, if you continue to ignore your goals and desires, you are actively telling yourself that you don't respect yourself. You do not take your art seriously. Worse than that, you lose your ability to trust yourself. The trust is broken when you say you're going to do the work but again and again and again you ghost yourself.

Say you go to an exhibition and see an awe-inspiring collection of photography. It motivates you. You decide it's time. You want to do what they're doing. You tell yourself you're going to get up early tomorrow morning, go on a walk, take some pictures and start an Instagram account to share your work. Incredible. The problem is that you've said you're going to do this a dozen times before and have never followed through. Or you did it once and never bothered to do anything with the images you took. Doubt creeps in. You don't trust yourself. You've not shown up for yourself in the past, so why would you show up tomorrow? The initial warm glow of the idea dims. In its place is a sinking mistrust and anger at yourself. You know you're not going to follow through. The trust is broken. The cycle continues.

REBUILDING TRUST

It's clear from years of research on procrastination that the most powerful way to motivate yourself is to have a strong sense of purpose or curiosity in what you're doing – intrinsic motivation, in other words. Unfortunately, if you've had a pattern of procrastination in the past, it will probably be difficult to access your intrinsic motivation. You will be in too much pain and emotional dysregulation to connect with curiosity.

The first step is proving to yourself that you can show up in your own name. This cannot be done through some big, grand gesture. This isn't about yet again promising yourself that today you'll write five thousand words, today you'll finish the painting in the garage, today you'll complete your whole website and put your clothing line up for sale.

As I've talked about before, I often witness creatives trying to solve the pain of procrastination with the grand gesture. Goal setting, especially big goal setting, gives us a massive dopamine hit; it combats all those negative feelings you've been having about your inability to show up properly. But it rarely works. It certainly never works consistently. To rebuild trust, you need to do something super-duper unsexy. You need to start very, very small.

That is what the two-week reset challenge is all about: small, consistent, creative touchpoints you can engage with regularly. Touchpoints that will help you rebuild your trust in yourself.

Once you've done the reset, you can start thinking about how you want your creative life to look in perpetuity. Do you want to go back to grand gestures? Or do you want to complete small, achievable tasks that will continue

I TRUST MY COMMITMENT TO MY ART

to build the relationship with yourself? Sit with your guitar and play for five minutes before dinner each night. Get out your pens, put them on your desk, and doodle with your cup of tea. Commit to writing one hundred words a day or reading three pages of research. Then acknowledge what you've done. Remind yourself that you are the sort of person who keeps the promises you make to yourself. Start to get rid of the dread.

I know it doesn't feel incredible to set a 'spend ten minutes every day knitting' goal, but when you achieve that small goal, a little bit of that trust is rebuilt, and when you've knitted every day for five days in a row, that's something to be proud of. When you hit day thirty and you've knitted for an accumulated three hundred-ish minutes, you might just start believing that this is the real deal and that perhaps you're going to show up tomorrow to do the exact same thing. The relationship heals; your faith in yourself starts to return. Go slower. Be kinder to yourself. Give yourself a fair chance. This is how you become a successful creative.

AFTER WE REBUILD TRUST, WE CAN REBUILD CURIOSITY

Once you've built that trust back up, you can begin to rediscover those feelings of curiosity and purpose that initially attracted you to art.

Our society treats curiosity like inspiration: something that must come naturally or it doesn't come at all. That isn't true. You can and you must actively foster curiosity in your life. And now that you have demonstrated that you can trust your own word, it is time to cultivate curiosity and a sense of purpose to propel you into long-term creativity. That's what we are really after: long-term creativity. You are here to create until you're done. *Done* done. Capital *D* done. (Dead.)

When you find yourself wanting to avoid your creativity, try to find the puzzle, the question you want to answer. Try to remember why you started making art in the first place. Cultivate curiosity.

Questions to invoke curiosity:

- How could my art support my personal growth?
- How could I be one of the best in my field?
- How could I surprise myself with this project?
- How could I use my craft to incite political change?
- How could I use only things from my recycling bin to make a sculpture of my dog?
- Could I make this three times bigger?
- Could I make this three times smaller?
- What would happen if I . . .
- Who killed her? (This is the question I ask when I write my murder mysteries.)
- Why did it not work last time?

These questions are here to provoke your curiosity. Let them lead you forward; let them seduce you back to your art.

WHEN YOU PROCRASTINATE, YOU DESERVE COMPASSION

You are the sort of person who shows up for your art. But that doesn't mean you won't procrastinate. How you treat yourself when you eventually screw up is the crucial, end-of-chapter conversation. We've already discussed it a bit in the two-week reset challenge, but this isn't the sort of thing that should be said only once. A lot of people won't commit to their creativity because they are so afraid of how they will treat themselves when they fail, procrastinate or disappoint themselves. They are so terrified of the way they treat themselves when they fail, they end up living an artless life.

When you procrastinate, you deserve compassion. That's a rebellious and revolutionary sentence. We perform better when we are treated compassionately.

We perform worse when we are treated worse. Stop pretending that the tirades your inner critic goes on when you procrastinate are useful. They are detrimental. They are making you a worse artist. You don't deserve them.

I mother myself when I procrastinate. I treat myself like a tiny baby child, and it works. (Jerry Seinfeld famously does this too.) That's not to say I don't get frustrated. I do. But I recover with a mothering voice. Here's an example from a 2019 journal entry, when I was working on my book *Maude*:

> I have spent the last three days straight doing anything other than writing my book. Every time I sit down to write, I feel overwhelmed and I don't even know where to start. There is too much to change. I feel like a fraud. I feel lazy. I haven't even been procrastinating with anything productive, I've just been screwing around.
>
> Take a deep breath. It's okay. What you're doing isn't easy and it is okay that you struggle. This is a journey. Your worth isn't dependent on your productivity. Your worth isn't dependent on what you do in the day. You are magic even when you struggle. And no amount of 'productivity' changes that.
>
> I trust that we will return to Maude and that we are able to coax her out of this confusion and do the work that needs to be done, but we will approach her gently, with a big cup of tea and a soft heart. There is no reason to stress or be angry at ourselves. All is happening exactly as it should.

I am coddling myself, in the best way. *Maude* eventually became *Regrettably, I Am About to Cause Trouble*, one of my most beloved books. Of course, I got her written, and of course I published her. I got there because of the compassion I dared to give myself.

You must find the language of compassion that your inner critic needs. You must figure out how to talk yourself down from the 'you're lazy and don't deserve to make art' ledge. Do you need to be spoken to like a child? Do you need to be firmly reminded of your worth? Figure out what you need. Practise talking to yourself or writing to yourself with compassion. It will feel uncomfortable for most of us, but with time, it will change everything.

There is nothing wrong with you.

You are not broken. Procrastination is part of this journey.

Discover what you are running from. Rebuild the trust. Find your curiosity and your purpose, and when you still inevitably end up in avoidance, shower yourself with understanding and love.

PROCRASTINATION PROMPTS

There is so much to unpack with our relationship to productivity and procrastination. We live in a world that conflates worth with output. It is incredibly hard to separate ourselves from these narratives, so I need you to be gentle with yourself as you navigate these prompts. There is much healing to be done.

1. **Do you need to forgive yourself for past procrastination patterns?** Do you need to let go of resentment/hate/anger that you are harbouring against yourself? Do you need to apologise for the way you have spoken to yourself in the past? In this prompt I want you to write a forgiveness/apology letter to yourself, letting yourself off the hook for all the times you've avoided your art. You deserve compassion, space, room to mess up. Let's make space for our creative journey by letting the guilt go.

2. **How have you been taught that you should show up as a creative?** What narratives are you harbouring about how much you *should* be creating? Do you feel that you SHOULD be creating daily? Or you SHOULD create

only very big projects? Notice any narratives around how you're 'meant' to create and ask yourself, *Is this how I want to create?*

3. **How do you define the following words and phrases?**
    - Successful creative practice
    - A good day of creating
    - Consistency
    - Productivity

Once you've defined them, examine them for your attitudes toward procrastination. Is there a different way to define them, one that better serves you and your art? If so, rewrite them.

I GRIEVE
ALL THE ART
NOT MADE
BECAUSE OF
PERFECTIONISM.

ON PERFECTIONISM

Note: there are ten spelling and grammatical errors in this chapter. Have fun finding them.

Perfectionism is the oldest trick in the artist's handbook. 'If I am going to do something as scary as create art, I'm going to bypass the vulnerability and potential for failure by being absolutely without fault'. It makes so much sense. What a clever way to avoid all the potential pain of being a creative! How ironic and cruel that perfectionism masquerades as a cure-all but is actually the root of so much suffering and pain for creatives.

I want to decimate any notion that perfectionism will help you. You think that perfectionism will push you, get you to the front of the pack. You believe that perfectionism is the personality flaw you really want. You've been taught that perfectionism is the ultimate humblebrag. This is dangerous. Perfectionism not only stops you creating anything in the first place, it also leads to lower-quality art in the long run. Worse, it leads to deeply unhappy artists.

It's almost impossible to convince a dyed-in-the-wool perfectionist that their favourite virtue is actually a vice because the perfectionist narrative is self-fullfilling. You tell yourself, *If I am a perfectionist, I can eliminate randomness, guarantee my success, escape failure.*

And then if it works out for you, you can credit perfectionism for your success. If it doesn't work out, you can say, *Well, I just wasn't perfect enough. I will be more perfect next time.*

Whatever happens, you see it as proof that you must be perfect. It's why perfectionism is so seductive. Once it latches on, it's almost impossible to get rid of it without a profound reframe.

This chapter is the profound reframe. I need you to know that no matter what your creative goals are, whether you want to have a joyful private practice of making stuff, or whether you want to obtain mastery of your craft and connect with millions, you can do it without perfectionism. You must do it without perfectionism, otherwise art will become the enemy.

Perfectionism slows down creativity because it is inextricably linked with procrastination. Perfectionism creates a terrible relationship between art and artist because you can never fulfil your own expectations. Perfectionism stops creatives from being witnessed because you're never good enough to be seen. Perfectionism cockblocks artists from satisfaction, joy, delight, purpose. I want you free of it. You are too important. You have too much to give. Your art is too precious to be tarnished by the expectation of its being constantly, consistently perfect.

I can't have you finish this book and think, *Yeah, perfectionism is dicey, but the way I demand 'greatness' from myself is completely different and totally fine*. It isn't. You have no idea how much you have to give and gain when you let go of perfectionism. So I hate to really put the knife in, but I am about to describe every single way I've ever seen perfectionism hurt creativity.

PERFECTIONISM AND PROCRASTINATION

Perfectionism is one of the main causes of procrastination. Remember in the last chapter, when I asked you what you were running away from? A lot of artists are running away from the feeling of being imperfect. A lot of us have been taught that we are only lovable when we are infallible, we are only worthy when we are excelling. But art demands mess, mistakes and failure. So instead of creating, we run. We avoid. We live an artless life.

Perfectionism has robbed us of world-changing art. It has stopped – I'm just going to go ahead and say – billions of artists throughout history from

Having very high standards doesn't make you work harder or achieve more. It paralyses you and keeps you small.

creating. Art that could have been was obliterated with just that little whisper, '*I dont think you're good enough to do this*'. You might be familiar. You might be the artist who hasn't made any art yet. If so, I see you, creative. It's time to understand how perfectionism is causing chronic procrastination and has been holding you back.

Below are some of the perfectionist narratives that cockblock artists from starting to create:

- You spend years researching your creative projects but never graduate to creating. The perfectionist story: you need to be an expert on the topic before beginning.

- You are waiting until your kids are grown because they'd distract you too much now. Or you are waiting until you have a studio to begin painting. Or you are waiting for lots of free time until you begin writing. The perfectionist story: you need the perfect environment to create.

- You've always wanted to play the piano, but you 'sucked' at music in school and have therefore decided that you are 'not musical enough to start'. The perfectionist story: you need to be naturally talented at something to pursue it.

Perfectionism is a defence mecanism. These narratives are here to 'protect' you. But you don't need protecting from art. Art's the thing that's going to make you and your life sparkle.

PERFECTIONISM STOPS YOU FROM FINISHING OR SHARING WHAT YOU HAVE CREATED

We have a whole chapter on finishing your art, so I won't press the point too much here. But people with persistent perfectionist narratives are unlikely to finish projects, and are even less likely to share their art.

Here are a few ways I see it happen:

PERFECTIONISM WILL RUIN YOUR RELATIONSHIP WITH YOURSELF AND BLOCK YOU FROM YOUR BRILLIANCE.

- Every time you show up for your art, you disappoint yourself. Art becomes synonymous with disappointment, shame and not being enough. You either quit or lose your love for the craft.
- You have never had experience with 'marketing', so you don't bother advertising your art. You wouldn't be good at it, so what's the point! Your art is left unchampioned and unwitnessed.
- You don't share all of your art on social media because your Instagram is themed and branded, and some of your art doesn't fit the vibes.
- You never finish your art because finished means perfect, and you're not there yet (you never will be).
- Every time you come to create, you procrastinate because coming face-to-face with an imperfect work triggers a flight response.

Perfectionism will prevent important and profound works of art from being finished, from being witnessed. And even if you do push through the narratives and complete the projects, you will be left feeling not enough, exhausted and resentful toward your creations. It doesn't need to be this way. You deserve an easeful and joyful creative practice.

PERFECTIONISM HURTS THE QUALITY OF YOUR ART

Perfectionism is most famous for its relationship to procrastination; it stops you in your tracks and prevents you from starting, finishing, sharing. And of course, as we've just seen, it's well-deserved fame. But perfectionism also makes you a worse artist. Your skills and abilities are hindered by your perfectionism. You hold yourself back from mastery and development when you let perfectionist narratives direct your creative journey. Here are a few ways I've seen this play out:

PERFECTIONISM IS PLAYING DEFENCE, PROTECTING YOU FROM POTENTIAL FAILURE OR SHAME. IT'S TIME TO PLAY OFFENCE. CREATE VULNERABLY. CREATE TO CONNECT. CREATE TO MAKE AN IMPACT.

- You are constantly editing, reworking, rereading, never letting yourself move on until you've *perfected* it. The process is expensive. You waste so much time and energy when you do this. You could've used those resources to create so much more, to explore your art in new ways, to become better. You could have been prolific, but instead you asked yourself to be perfect.
- You overedit your art, taking away some of that raw, initial magic.
- You never get to learn from mistakes, because every time you make a mistake, you spiral into narratives about not being good enough, therefore stunting your growth as an artist.
- You burn out before you can complete your art, because of the exhaustion of having to show up perfectly.
- Your art is guarded and doesn't reflect who you are, just how you want to be perceived.

People assume that successful and talented artists get that way because they demand perfection of themselves, but you fulfil your creative potential when you befriend imperfection. Mastery evades the perfectionist.

I shared the above sentence on social media the other day, and here are three of many similar comments I received.

'Yeah! But not for Beyoncé!'

'You forgot about Taylor Swift, she's the exception!'

'What about Davinci [sic]?'

We live in a culture that believes exceptional art requires perfectionism, when it's literally the opposite. Da Vinci was a famous tinkerer and experimenter. He designed a helicopter that would have been unable to take off if he'd ever got around to making it. People think Da Vinci was a perfectionist because he left a trail of unfinished projects and artworks. The other side to the story is that Da Vinci was an experimenter, someone who tried things, and when they didn't work, he didn't give up, he tried something else. He used failure and imperfection as a stepping stone. I bet Beyoncé and Taylor have made shitty art on the way to making art that deeply resonates. There is no other way they could have gotten to where they are now. We need to stop crowning these artists as perfectionists. They are not perfect, and that is why they're brilliant.

PERFECTIONISM IMPACTS YOUR RELATIONSHIP WITH YOURSELF

This is my final and most important list. Because even if you do manage to find wild *success* as a perfectionist (this happened in spite of your perfectionism, mind you), what you will not find is joy, fulfilment and a sense of enough-ness.

Here is what happens when you demand only the very best from yourself:

- You become the antagonist, the unfair disciplinarien, the villain of your own life.
- You deprive yourself of deep joy and delight.
- You will lose your love of art.
- You never know your potential.
- You constantly compare yourself with others, and constantly find yourself wanting.
- You will never feel enough.

Imperfection is not the threat. Perfection is. Can you see that now?

THERE IS NO RULE BOOK FOR YOUR ART

It's not your fault that you turned to perfectionism to protect yourself, but it's your responsibility to begin a new path. One of mess, of play, of your own rules. You've been creating through the lens of others, through the external rules of perfectionism; now it's time to rebel. Screw those rules. You were never made to obey them. They've kept you too small. We get to set the terms of our creative process. There's no rule book. This is your divine practice, and it is entirely up to you. that's terrifying. We're taught to follow rules, to listen to other people's deadlines, to stay in line. But if we are to thrive as artists, we must listen to our own voice, realise our own rhythms, pave our own way.

How do you like to create? At what pace do you like to create? What are some reasonable goals and standards you could have for yourself that are achievable?

You may have listened to your inner critic or the external world for so long that you have no idea what the answers are to these questions. You may not know what your rhythms, processes and desires are. And if you don't know them, you can't even begin to think about honouring them. That's okay – we can start here.

It's time to find your own internal rhythms and processeses.

Healing your perfectionist tendencies means listening to your body. It means getting back in touch with how you like to work. How can you rediscover your rhythms? How can you discover your creative alignment? It will be a process of trial and error. You must notice how you are currently creating and recognise what is working and what isn't. I also want you to pay attention to the rules you are consciously or unconsciously following. Do you always have to create at a certain time of day, or when you have at least X hours to do so? Do you always have a deadline or never have a deadline? Do you only have to create art that would be deemed highbrow?

Notice the rules you are following, and rebel against the ones that are rooted in perfectionism. Rebel against the ones that don't serve you. Rebel against rules just because you're curious to see what happens. Notice your perfectionist voice when you do so. Be kind to it. It's frightened. Then remind it that you are making art on your own terms now. Only then will you form new stories, new patterns, new practices. This is radical permission-giving, allowing yourself to practise your art in ways that might seem strange, require boundaries or get weird looks. It is effort and discipline. It is a commitment to you.

THE FREEDOM OF SUBJECTIVITY

We have been conditioned to believe that art is objective, like a marathon or the score of a football game. But artists are not like athletes, we cannot win gold, we cannot beat other artists. We cannot come first. Creating to be the best is exhausting and a waste of energy. It's exhausting striving to be objectively perfect in a subjective, messy realm. Even if you win an Oscar or come first in a dance competition, thats still subjective. People will still think you didn't deserve the Oscar or that someone else danced better. The mythical standard of perfection isn't real.

I need you to stop pushing so hard and just create in your way, because there is no other way. I need you to focus on your own unique brand of magic. This is how we take the defensiveness of perfectionism and transform it into active, vibrant creative energy. You have something so unique to give. If you choose to hold it in – it will die with you. You need to stop focusing on protecting yourself and start focusing on the potential you hold. The idiosyncracies, the weird choices, the mistakes, the way you infuse your life experiences into your creations. That's all *your* magic. That's what you need to focus on.

HOW DO I FIND MY OWN UNIQUE MAGIC?

This is a big question, one that we will look at in detail in the finding-your-voice chapter. Discovering your own brand of creative power takes time and courage. The only thing I know for sure is that you won't find your own unique brand of magic if you are being a perfectionist. Perfectionist creating is a conservative way of making art. It's playing safe and small. You can't discover your treasure trove of weird and wonderful ways when you are trying to be infallible. Discovering your own unique magic requires experimentation. Creative experimentation abhors perfection. Let the mess in.

ARTISTS ARE NOT LIKE ATHLETES. WE CANNOT WIN GOLD, WE CANNOT BEAT OTHER CREATIVES, WE CANNOT COME FIRST. SPORT IS OBJECTIVE; ART IS SUBJECTIVE. CREATING TO BE THE BEST IS A WASTE OF ENERGY. INSTEAD, CREATE TO CONNECT TO THE PEOPLE WHO NEED YOU, BECAUSE THEY ARE OUT THERE. CREATE IN YOUR OWN WAY, BECAUSE THERE IS NO RIGHT WAY. TAKE THE PRESSURE OFF AND FOCUS ON YOUR OWN UNIQUE BRAND OF MAGIC.

MAKE SHITTY ART A CREATIVE PRACTICE

I want to take it a step further. Beyond mess. Beyond experimentation. I want to invite shitty art into our creative practice. To find our own unique magic and to truly thwart perfectionism, we must have a relationship with making bad art. I love shitty art. It has been transformative for me as an author. Allowing yourself to make 'bad' art regularly will let you and your nervous system know that it is safe to make art that isn't good. But you must do it regularily. Bad art must be a practice. Spend ten minutes before your next creation session and specifically ask yourself to make something terrible. Buy bad tools or make something with only half the needed materials. Give yourself the explicit instruction: make something bad. Your body has to learn that it's safe to not reach perfection. No teacher will yell at you. No parent will throw what you've done in the bin. You are allowed to be messy, you're allowed to be mediocre. It's okay if it doesn't work. You will soon realise all this art you consider to be bad is just a holy and divine stepping stone to your next piece of art, your next idea, your next iteration. It is mandatory and beautiful.

WHAT EXACTLY IS SHITTY ART? ARE YOU SURE IT'S STRICTLY NECESSARY?

In 2019, I was reported for a social media post I made about shitty art. My Instagram account was restricted for bullying and hate speech. I ended up speaking to the woman who reported me and she explained her views. She believed there is no such thing as shitty art. That all art is good art. And my belief in, nay, my love of shitty art was degrading to artists.

You don't have to get behind my reclamation of bad art. If you don't want to call any of your art shitty, that's okay. I understand that because art is subjective, there really isn't such a thing as shitty art. But, in the eye of the artist, sometimes we make stuff that we really don't like. And that is the art I am choosing to call shitty art.

I cannot expect to love everything I make. That is unfair. It is a symptom

HOW TO DEFEAT PERFECTIONISM:

MAKE SHITTY ART.

DO IT EVERY DAY.

of perfectionism. I also don't need to pretend that everything I make is worth sharing. I frequently write really bad stuff! This particular chapter has been the nightmare of this book. That's safe. It's all good.

I believe that making 'bad art' is simply part of the process. It doesn't speak to your skill set. It doesn't speak to how successful you're going to be. It's just something that happens when you make art. In fact, it's something that MUST happen if you want to make 'good art'. Shitty art is how you find your voice. It's how you discover what it is you want to create. It's how you discover your style. You get so much information when you make something you don't like. You can use that information to become a master of your craft. You can use that information to make art that has an impact. Stop trying to skip the shitty art.

HOW CAN I MAKE A PRACTICE OF SHITTY ART?

There are lots of ways we can purposefully integrate shitty art into our creative lives.

For example, I am not allowed to edit when I am writing the first draft of any book. I am not even allowed to reread. It means I can brain dump all my ideas onto the page with speed and flow. This method of writing results in a lot of shitty art.

I know writers who write with the brightness turned down on their laptops so they can't see what they're writing. Sure, sometimes they have written whole chapters in caps lock, but there is magic in making without monitoring. River Wintergreen, a visual artist, often draws with their eyes shut.

Consider having a play session once a week, where you just let yourself create as though you're a child again. Honour and act on cringey, strange art ideas, even if you're 99 per cent sure it will make shit art. Good. We make shit art around here.

After you've made your shitty art, instead of shaming yourself and destroying the evidence, display the crap and take ownership of it. Why don't you frame your worst pieces of art? Make a gallery of your failures. Make a playlist of half-finished crappy songs you've written. Have a document of comically terrible sentences. You don't have to publicly share your least favourite creations, but when we proudly own the fact that we make shitty art, we bring it out of the shadows of shame. Shame cannot thrive when it is in the light. If we can honour, even delight in, the crap we are rewriting the belief that perfect art is the only way to please.

(As a side note, River ended up taking their favourite eyes-closed drawings and turning them into a calendar. It's delightful and I bought two of them! Shitty art doesn't mean you are a shitty artist. It is the foundation of great work.)

This chapter was the shittiest of the book to write. I have so many feelings and things to say about perfectionism that I got lost and confused, and made some shitty art. I cried about it. I got annoyed. But the perfectionist chapter needs to be imperfect. It wouldn't be right otherwise. So I take a deep breath, exhale, and say this is enough. I trust that even though I'm not entirely happy with this chapter, there are magical and important words here. I let go

PERFECTIONISM PROMPTS

In this chapter, we discussed the perils of perfectionism and the ways we can reclaim our mess. But we didn't get a chance to look at why the perfectionist narratives were there in the first place. Initially, I wrote several pages about the perils of our education systems, societal expectations, rejection sensitivity, our parents... all the many reasons why artists develop debilitating perfectionism. But the truth is that you need to unpack this part of the journey yourself. Perfectionism is rooted in your past, in your experiences. I cannot tell you why you are a perfectionist, but I can ask questions that will hopefully lead you to understanding. And with understanding come compassion and patience and space.

1. **When has perfection or excellence been required of you in the past?** You'll want to look at two of the main culprits here – how you were educated and how your parents raised you. Were you in a culture that celebrated achievement above all else? For example, I went to a school where students were ranked from best to worst in performance within each class.

2. **What are your experiences of 'falling short' of other people's expectations?** How were you treated? Is it how you treat yourself now when you fall short of your own expectations? Interestingly, you might want to look at how parental figures treated themselves when they fell short of their own expectations. For example, when your parent burned the dinner, did they get very angry with themselves? Do you now mirror that behaviour?

3. **What is your experience with mess in your life?** Have you been allowed to be messy? Consider your bedroom, schoolbooks, appearance, etc. Were you policed for how you showed up in the world? How do you respond to that now? Historically, how have you responded to that?

4. **What is your experience with rejection?** Detail standout experiences of rejection from your past. How did you respond? How did others around you respond? How does your relationship with rejection affect you now?

ON JEALOUSY AND COMPARISON

When we aren't trying to make perfect art, we are sneaking a peek at the artist sitting next to us, wondering why we aren't as good as they are. In this chapter, we are going to look at jealousy and comparison. Artists are susceptible to these two experiences because of the vulnerability of our work. No artist completely evades the temptation to compare or the feeling of wanting what someone else has. It is a normal part of the creative journey.

FOLLOW YOUR JEALOUSY

Jealousy can be such a stagnant feeling. You want what they have. You don't have what they have. There is nothing to be done. Jealousy can leave us feeling powerless and without agency. But I want to utilise this emotion. Jen Sincero writes that 'jealousy is a road map'. I read the sentence and felt immediately empowered. Jealousy can take us places. Jealousy can be our compass. It can be an insight into our creative vision and desires. It can point us in the direction of our creative dreams.

Jealousy is also an opportunity for us to question our desires. Do I actually want what they have? Or do I simply feel like I *should* have what they have? Is this about cultural expectations or my innermost creative desires?

The problem is that jealousy is a taboo emotion. It's hard for us to use

Jealousy is a sign that you know where you want to go. It is an invitation to claim what you want. It is a call to action. **Take it.**

jealousy to guide us when it isn't socially appropriate to talk about it. Jealousy is culturally depicted as villainous, the green-eyed monster, a dirty and polluting emotion to experience. But jealousy is something we all experience!

To break the ice from the get-go, I'm going to confess some of the jealousies I've experienced on my own journey. We don't need to hide jealousy in shame. In the shame, jealousy festers and becomes useless, dark and toxic.

An inexhaustive list of artists I've been jealous of:

- Flex Mami. Ghanaian Australian author and artist. Flex has a way with words that is so humorous and witty that every time I read even just the text in a benign Instagram story of hers, I am annoyed and jealous that I didn't write it myself. She has a charisma and magnetism that is unlike anyone else I've seen.
- Candice Brathwaite. Her words, her aura, her style. The way she makes content lights me up. And I regularly think, *I wish but I could never.*
- Julia Cameron. Mother of all creatives. I compare myself a lot to this author. Am I articulating this point as well as Mama Julia does? Should I be more gentle and spiritual like Julia? Am I a mere shadow compared with this incredible creative?
- [Unnamed author who got publishing deals when I was being rejected.] This one was a deep feeling of unhealthy jealousy. [Brilliant author] writes wonderful fantasy novels and was kicking off and making waves as I was being rejected by hundreds of publishers. Why her? Why her? Why her? It was all-consuming jealousy.

I could've let these jealousies fester into something dark. Instead, I let them guide me.

I have taken huge inspiration from Flex. She gave me permission to let my humour shine in public, something I had previously been holding back on. Candice kicked off my journey with fashion and being bold with my visual choices. She inspires me to wear bright colours and to take care with the details.

My jealousy of and comparison with Julia Cameron forced me to come to terms with the fact that I don't want my writing to be like hers. Her wisdom guides me, but my words and style and thoughts are my own. My downright unhealthy journey with the jealousy of [unnamed author] has been a harder one to alchemise, but it sank me deeper into the knowledge that I want my writing to have an audience, that I tell stories to share them with people. It reminded me that I was on the path, striving for something real, even if I had not achieved it yet.

COMPARISON

Jealousy is when you want what they have. Comparison is when you look at what you have and put it side by side with what they have. Jealousy can be used as a compass, pointing directly at what it is you desire. Comparison, on the other hand, can be disorienting and distracting, fertile ground for cruelty. It can be a playground for the inner critic. It is incredibly difficult to use comparison to elevate yourself as an artist.

As I wrote this book, I ducked into some of the other big books on creativity. I did so with the purest intentions, to 'get ideas' or to 'just look at how they do it'. But every time I did it, it just served to confuse me and distract me from my voice and vision. Similarly, I have a habit of comparing myself to . . . myself. I've been looking at a lot of my older writing and comparing my past work to what I'm doing now. Again, it's only been disorienting. I am strangely vulnerable to the narrative that you were so good back then, but it's all in the past. You're like Benjamin Button but you're just getting worse at writing as you get older. That part of me is afraid. She's creating something vulnerable, and the stakes seem too high, she's terrified we won't be able to do a good job. She needs to be taken care of.

HOW DO WE TAKE CARE OF OURSELVES WHEN WE ARE IN CYCLES OF COMPARISON?

I know creatives who choose to isolate themselves from art that triggers comparison. They cleanse their feeds of the art, and they avoid spaces with artists who bring about feelings of comparison. I stopped reading other creativity books when I wrote the first draft of this book. I've also banned any rereading of old work for the time being. I am protecting myself by keeping my inner critic out of spaces where she is vulnerable to having a comparison meltdown.

That being said, I also believe that if we intentionally foster a growth mindset, we can use comparison to spur us on. Carol Dweck popularised the term *growth mindset* and has done some brilliant research and writing about it. In her book *Mindset*, Dweck explains that a growth mindset is the belief that your abilities can be developed through dedication and work, and that having talent or a natural aptitude is a bonus but not necessary for excellence. This perspective on life encourages a love for learning and a curiosity about our own potential. Alternatively, when we adopt a fixed mindset, we believe we are doomed to constantly be less than other artists who we perceive as being more talented than us – a pale shadow of other artists everywhere.

With a growth mindset, we can use comparison to become better artists. Comparison can lead to striving and curiosity. For example, I'm not yet at the level of X, but I think I can get there by doing Y. Or this person's style is a bit like mine, but I think I can put a different spin on it by doing Z. When we start asking questions, it can lead us deeper into our own creative process.

WHEN SOMEONE IS MAKING SOMETHING SIMILAR TO YOURS

Why is it so upsetting to see someone doing the same thing as you? In my last year of school, I elected to do a subject that included a major creative project.

I chose to write a ten-thousand-word short story. On brand, though I didn't know it yet, I wrote a story about Queen Elizabeth I and her lover Robert Dudley. Halfway through this venture, I realised Philippa Gregory, famous and mega-bestselling historical fiction author, had just come out with a book with an eerily similar plot to my own. Seventeen-year-old Amie was distraught. I remember crying in the bookshop to my mum. 'What's the point! What's the point if Philippa has done it already?'

Mum was kind enough to take my distress seriously, but, retrospectively, I laugh. It was a school project. I wasn't exactly fighting for bookshelf space with Philippa. But the thought of someone else writing a similar story to mine filled me with a real and terrible distress. It made me think there was no point in continuing with the project. It can be deeply upsetting to watch another artist do something similar to you. Especially if they have more resources, receive recognition or are further along in their journey.

Creatives love to be unique. We have a thirst for individuality. We must be different.

First, the bad news: You cannot be entirely innovative. People will make things that look like your thing. People will create things that overlap with what you're doing.

But I also have beautiful news for you: You are entirely and completely, effortlessly unique. You don't need to get any weirder (unless you want to), you don't need to be deliberately different or to try to do the opposite of what everyone else is doing. Unless you are literally copying someone else's exact artwork, you are unique. I know this is a very wishy-washy, new-age thing to say. It feels like something parents get derided for saying to their children. But I mean this in a really practical sense. Two writers working from exactly the same outline will write two different books. I would wager the books would be so different that many people would be completely oblivious to their shared origins. The same goes for two musicians working off the same prompts, two artists painting the same scene, two actors reading from the same script. They will all, naturally, do something unique.

In the past, when I had a new idea, I would obsessively research whether

OTHER PEOPLE WILL HAVE MADE ART SIMILAR TO YOUR ART. IT IS NOT A CAUSE FOR PANIC. IT ISN'T A THREAT. IT'S PROOF OF MARKET. THERE'S ROOM FOR YOU.

anyone had done anything like that before (perhaps a hangover from my year twelve assignment). As soon as I realised that someone had dabbled in the arena I wanted to create in, the 'what's the point' narrative would begin to play. 'What's the point? What can I give that's not already been given?' Inevitably, I would then call my partner, James, into my study to declare that there was no point in creating anything ever again because someone's already done it and done it better and I should now become an accountant.

Then James would remind me: 'Their creations are not a threat. It's proof that people are hungry for what you're making. It's evidence that there is interest and intrigue. Now you get to infuse your own unique magic into this conversation. And I can guarantee no one has seen this perspective before. Also, please don't become an accountant, it would be a massive net bad for the world'.

I moved through a lot of anger when my novel *The Rules Upheld by No One* was rejected left, right and centre for having a 'modern voice'. Publishers thought historical fiction with a modern voice would confuse readers. I thought gatekeepers were wrong and that readers were smart enough to understand what I was trying to do. The rage intensified when this very genre of anachronistic historical fiction began popping up in shows like *The Great* and *Dickinson*. Now I honour my frustration. At the time, though, it felt horrible. It probably set me back from self-publishing that book by at least a year. It took me a long time to reframe my outrage. I eventually got to a point where I could see that these shows were just proof that there was an appetite for what I was doing, even if gatekeepers couldn't see it. There was an audience out there that wanted historical heroines who curse and don't finish every sentence with 'verily'. And, what do you know, I was right! Anachronistic historical TV series didn't cancel out the viability of my book. Several people have compared my books with those shows, and not a single one accused me of stealing or copying from them.

Creatives, if someone is doing something similar to you and it's doing well, it isn't a threat, it's auspicious – this is a conversation that wants to happen, and you get to be a part of it, in your own entirely unique way.

THE SATURATED MARKET

The next step after we see someone doing the same thing we want to do is to declare the market saturated. They're starting a podcast + you want to start a podcast + there seem to be lots of podcasts = saturated market = no point in starting your podcast. And yet, of the 4 million plus podcasts out there, only about 5 per cent regularly upload an episode. There are more people listening now too. In 2018, 26 per cent of Americans reported listening to a podcast at least once a month. Now that figure is 42 per cent, or about 120 million people. The market is growing! And only a small fraction of podcasts are taking it seriously! The saturated market statements usually fall apart when you dig a little deeper.

Humans are prone to all sorts of cognitive biases that make this seem worse. We're really bad at accurately gauging how popular something is. Something called the availability bias means we have a tendency to overestimate the popularity or frequency of something if we can readily recall a specific example of it. So it seems like everyone has a podcast because we know a friend who started one.

Or take, for example, vampire books. Yes, they appear to be everywhere because you can easily recall a popular vampire series from the mid-2000s. It's been done. What's the point? Well, this isn't a boom-and-bust cycle. You might be surprised to learn that vampires have been consistently popular for the past fifty years. There's a great *Slate* article from 2009 by Christopher Beam and Chris Wilson titled 'When Have We Not Been in the Midst of a Vampire Craze?' The answer is basically, never. Sure, there have been some huge peaks in popularity, but most of the time, people seem to be interested in vampires.

Whether it's podcasts or vampire novels or art of your own particular genre, I'm going to say something now that you might find hard to believe: the market is basically never saturated, you just need to find a way to connect with your audience.

Art is profoundly different from most other things businesses try to sell

ART IS NOT TOASTER

you. If people are raving fans of a certain type of art, their appetite for art is effectively infinite. I made a video about this once, and it was really good. Let me try to reenact it for you. I point at a toaster. I point at a fridge. I point at a TV. We really *need* only one of these items. If there are too many toaster companies, there will be a saturated market, because we want only one toaster per household.

Art isn't like this.

The video continues: I point at my bookshelf, which easily homes several hundred books. I point at my walls, which are filled with visual art. I open Netflix: literally thousands of films. We have an insatiable appetite for art, which means the market is not capped, which means there is room for you.

I know it seems like there are so many podcasts, and sure, there are loads of people writing horny fairy books right now because they're popping off on TikTok, but we have an insatiable appetite for those things. Is there some magical number of horny fantasy novels that the Kindle Store can reach where suddenly everyone just stops reading them? If a lot of other people are making something similar to yours, it can make it hard to stand out. But that also means there is a huge market for what you're making. You need to figure out how to connect with that market. That is a big task, one for a whole new book, but begin asking yourself questions like: Where does your audience hang out? What online platforms do they spend time on? Where would you find them in real life? How can you create community with them? How can you build a sense of trust with them? How can you let them know that your art is there for them to buy? Marketing your art is a big journey of choosing yourself and being your own biggest fan, but remember, people love to part with their money for art they love, for art they think will scratch an itch that is, essentially, unscratchable.

ART IS NOT TOASTER

The reason *art* feels like *toaster* is because of gatekeepers. It is difficult to saturate a committed audience's desire for art. It is, however, easy to overwhelm the gatekeepers' ability to satisfy that audience. Publishers can take on only so many novels a year. Film studios have only so much money to invest in projects. And the second there's a little dip in popularity or competition starts to come for their market share, gatekeepers will cut and run. Their quarterly performance metrics are at risk! If we want to be chosen by big businesses, then, yes, we are looking at a market that is capped.

But the *art* market isn't capped. Or, at least, the cap is so high that it's almost not even worth thinking about. It's hard to spend more on horny fantasy books than you do on rent or groceries. And that's important to remember. I can publish my anachronistic historical fiction book by myself, and find my own audience, because even though publishers didn't have any more room for my art, the market was insatiable for it and ate it up.

We are moving into a world where creatives can take up space without big companies backing them. We have more agency and more power, and we have a market that is absolutely frothing for more art.

The saturated market isn't an excuse for not creating. Even if *art* was *toaster* and the market was 'full', you should still create your art, as there is so much more to gain from our art beyond its connection to our audience. But that's neither here nor there, because the art market can't be saturated. You don't need to be jealous, or to panic at the comparison between you and those artists who're doing something really similar to you. It's a good thing that they're creating something similar to yours. There is space for you. You're not too late. You're right on time.

COMPARISON WITH OTHER PEOPLE'S PROCESS

While we might be able to appreciate our art as unique and our own, we also have to watch out that we don't compare our creative process to others' as well.

We can get so fixated on how 'the greats' approach their art. We become obsessed with asking any artist we meet how they organise their days. How many words do they write? How long do they spend in the studio? What method do they use to get in character?

THE PAIN:
JEALOUSY.

THE SALVE:
CREATION.

The result is often that we find our own methods wanting, simply because they are different. They spend seven hours a day at their craft! I spend only half an hour! They use the expensive materials; I can afford only the ones made for kids. They have the best microphones, whereas mine were cheapest and I got them in a Black Friday sale.

There is nothing wrong with wanting to know how other people work, especially if you are not happy with your creative process and are looking to switch things up. As I previously mentioned, I'm not super concerned about you being jealous of other people's routines, because you can use that jealousy as a road map. I was extremely jealous of those who got to work full time at their craft for years. Again, I used it as my compass. The jealousy informed me of my desires.

The problem arises when we get in a pattern of comparison. Your creative output will be different from everyone else's. Your energy levels are unique. Your life circumstances are different too. The way you ideate, the way you craft, the way you finesse, the way you edit, the way you solve problems, the way you recover – they are all entirely unique to you. And comparing your process to someone else's is unfair and not useful.

In the past, I fell into the dangerous pattern of comparing my process to creatives I thought were harder workers than me. I would obsess over their full schedules and wonder, *Why aren't they exhausted? How can they be around so many people so often? How can they go from one event to the next? How can they take on so many projects at once? How are they so energetic? How do they stay up so late?* It made me think I wasn't made for creativity or any sort of creative success. I would obsessively compare my creative process to these extroverted, type A, seemingly unstoppable artists.

I had to remind myself that if I had tried to mimic what they did with their lives, not only would I hate my life, I would also be physically, mentally, spiritually broken. I am not made to have more than one big thing going on in a day. I am not made to be up past 9:00 p.m. I shouldn't write more than 1,500 words on a very, *very* good day, and usually I should write a lot fewer. I know this about myself, so why would I compare my process with that of someone who is entirely different from me?

I am leading a delightfully creative life not in spite of the fact that I honour my own rhythms and pace, but *because* I honour my rhythms and pace. This chronically tired and often unwell introvert is making an impact and enjoying creative abundance while honouring her body's needs.

The only way you are going to find creative joy and success is if you figure out how you like to create and then honour it, no matter what it looks like when you put it side by side with JLo's routine.

Remember: Your pace is holy. Your rhythm is holy. Your art is holy.

It's time to own it.

JEALOUSY AND COMPARISON PROMPTS

There is work to be done on this. Artists will always be vulnerable to jealousy and comparison, and it is up to us to make sure it does not tarnish our practice or poison our minds. Let's foster a growth mindset; let's use these resistances to become phenomenal artists.

1. **Who do you have a habit of comparing yourself with? Why?** Let's use this prompt to investigate what stories you are playing out in your mind about your own creativity. Why are you comparing yourself with them? Tread very gently here, it can be a sensitive topic.

2. **Were you compared with others when you were younger?** How did this play out? Parents comparing siblings is a good example of this.

3. **What stories does your comparison/jealousy reinforce?** For example: comparing myself with X validates my story that I will never be recognised / good enough / lovable / talented.

4. **What are the consequences of your relationship with jealousy and comparison?** Are they affecting your creative life?

5. **Can jealousy be a road map to your desires?** Does it reaffirm what it is you are working toward? OR does it not actually align with what you want? If not, why?

6. **Write down all the things that you are jealous of.** Look at the list, and answer the following questions:

    - Are your listed jealousies things that you personally desire for your own creative journey? Do you actually want these things for yourself? Or are they things you believe you should have?

    - If they are things you actually desire, are you on the path? Is your comparison and jealousy exacerbated because you are not taking action toward achieving these things? Is there a gap between what you are desiring and what you are doing?

    - If you are not taking action toward your goals, be gentle with yourself. Is this the source of the jealousy and comparison? What small, small action could you incorporate into your life that brings you closer to the things you desire?

    - If you are taking action toward your goals, take a moment to write about that, to remind yourself that you are on this sacred journey, doing all the things that are calling you.

    - If you found yourself looking at the list of jealousies and not actually wanting or being desirous of these things, what an incredibly potent discovery! Write about that. Let's get curious about why the jealousy and comparison are still rearing their heads. Is it because of the external validation the other person receives? Is it because of attention they receive? Is it because you feel like you deserve what they have, even if you don't want it? This is big work. Go slowly and try not to judge yourself.

7. **In this prompt, we're going to honour the pain, the unfairness, the ickiness of jealousy. And then we are stepping into our power.** This prompt has two parts. First, honour the pain of any jealousy or comparison you are currently feeling through a note to yourself:

For example, *I acknowledge the fact that X got a publishing contract, and their opportunity to speak at X event triggered immense jealousy. I honour my own pain. That was so hard to go through. It was a reasonable response to be upset, and it was reasonable to have thoughts about why this happened, and to question my own worth. I understand why I responded this way. I also acknowledge that a part of this situation was unfair. At the end of the day this was a lot of bad luck. Life just didn't do what I wanted it to do. And that is really hard. I can be sad.*

Next, honour the sanctity and uniqueness of your own journey through a note to yourself:

For example, *However, I honour the fact that this wasn't my path to take. I did all that I could. My path is unique. It is enchanted. It is different from all others. I am incomparable because of how unique I am, and I trust that all is unfolding as it must. When opportunities I desire are given to others, or when I watch others thrive, I acknowledge any jealousy I feel, but then I remind myself that I am STILL on the path to abundance and success. I trust my own path. I do not do things like they do. I do things my way, and it is going to pay dividends. There is space for both of us. There is space for me.*

ON BURNOUT

After chapters on procrastination, perfectionism, and jealousy and comparison, I think it is very apparent why artists are so vulnerable to burnout. You must take immaculate care of your mind and your body to prevent losing yourself to exhaustion. You might have already found your reserves failing, your inspiration waning and your belief in your creative journey fading. There are so many creative people who can't bring themselves to do what they are made for, because their bones are heavy with fatigue.

The good news is, art doesn't have to be hard and exhausting. You can learn to create with ease and restore your body and mind. You don't have to burn out.

WHAT IS BURNOUT?
WHAT DOES IT LOOK LIKE FOR CREATIVES?

Burnout is a state of emotional, physical and mental exhaustion, caused by excessive and prolonged stress. But let me describe the different ways it has manifested for me.

When I was working day jobs that I hated, desperately squeezing art into the in-between moments, burnout appeared as a deep-in-my-bones lethargy.

I couldn't get off the couch, not because of exhaustion, but because of apathy and lethargy to the whole experience of life. Everything took so much energy. My central nervous system was in a permanent freeze. I had no will to do anything. I was detached. It hardly mattered if it was art or if it was the mundane stuff of life; burnout took the zest for life out of me. Coming home after a day working at the café, nannying, being a receptionist or personal training, I would stare at my computer, trying to write and create, and I would feel totally empty and unmotivated. My eyes would get stuck on fixed points, and just moving them would feel agonisingly draining.

By the end of my first year working full time as a creative mentor, it was a whole different story. This burnout was different. I was no longer apathetic and lethargic. My life excited and fuelled me. I had so many ideas, and I had the motivation to create. But after a year of doing the things I loved, I started feeling a strange physical pain all over my body. An aching. Like I had pulled a lot of different muscles in the gym. Then came the overriding anxiety. This was new for me. I knew what it was like to be anxious about stuff. But I had never experienced the irrational narratives that started popping up, giving me huge rushes of adrenaline and making my heart hurt. With every pain in my body, my central nervous system would go into fight-or-flight mode. I was constantly dizzy. I could hardly breathe.

I was having panic attacks. Like so many others who have their first experience with panic attacks, I thought something was seriously wrong with me physically. It felt like my body was shutting down. But when I finally mustered up the courage to see health professionals, they all came back with the same thing: 'You're exhausted. Your body and mind are fatigued, and you're having panic attacks'. It took having a month off work to rest and recalibrate before the physical pain and mental anguish calmed down. But it is something I manage and am medicated for to this day.

I have experienced burnout in situations where I was creatively blocked and situations where I was creatively abundant. It doesn't matter what part of the journey you are on, artists are always vulnerable to burnout.

WHY ARE CREATIVES SO VULNERABLE TO BURNOUT?

I am about to collate a big list of all the ways I've seen artists burn out. But before I do that, I want to look at some of the core reasons why creative people are so very vulnerable to exhaustion.

SOCIETY DOESN'T GIVE YOU SPACE OR TIME FOR YOUR ART

You must carve out space and time for your art. Rebelliously. And then you must defend that space and time. This takes effort. It is exhausting, constantly fighting for your right to create. Not only are you balancing your family life, work life, electricity bills, tax forms, social life, health, unanswered group chats, water intake, pets, activism, etc. – you are also trying to carve out space for your art. You are living multiple entirely full lives all at once. And the Art Life is a big, big life. You've seen what it takes to be an artist. It requires so much work, not just on the craft but on yourself. If you aren't careful, it can be too much. If you are not strategic, if you don't have good boundaries, if you don't keep your ego in check, you will become overwhelmed. And art is nearly always the first thing to go. No one judges you for giving up your piano practice, but people have a thing to say when you give up your kids or, worse, don't file your taxes. Socially, art is the easiest sacrifice to make.

Constantly fighting for your right to make art, both with yourself and with those around you, is tiring. This isn't a small thing. Don't underestimate the toll it takes.

ART ASKS YOU TO FACE YOURSELF

I don't know this to be true, never having been an accountant myself, but my guess is that you probably don't have to come face-to-face with all your internal demons when you are doing accounting work. (Though I have seen some pretty messed-up parts of myself when I look at an Excel spreadsheet, so who knows.) Artists, on the other hand, can't face their work without facing

Exhaustion, busyness and burnout are not prerequisites for creative success.

themselves. Procrastination, as we have seen, will exhaust you. Your inner critic, who berates you every time you make a mistake, will wear you down. The way you don't believe you're worthy of joy in your life? That comes up when you paint or write or make music, for some reason. You can't use art to hide from the difficulties of life. Art is not a numbing mechanism. No, art exposes. Being an artist requires coming home to yourself, every time you create. And if we are still overwhelmed with narratives of perfectionism, impostor syndrome and creative shame, that can be exhausting.

Art is a bit like nuclear energy. It has the potential to power whole cities, but it also has the power to destroy, the potential to both heal and devastate.

ARTISTS TREAT THEIR CREATIVITY LIKE A CORPORATE JOB

When I first started taking my writing seriously, I decided I needed to work absurdly hard, to the point of breaking, to validate art as a form of 'real work'.

Society tells us that if we do something rewarding or fun for a living, we must suffer in other ways for it. After all, doing something useful and fulfilling should be its own reward. For teachers and nurses, this might take the form of poor pay and long hours. As artists, we internalise narratives like 'So you're going to play for a living? You're going to have a delightful job? One that you love? If so, you better have a miserable time doing it, you better be working harder than anyone'.

I tried writing and creating from nine to five, just like my 'real adult' friends. I pushed and pushed and pushed myself to mirror the corporate world. And then I broke. Because creative work doesn't behave like other work. At least, not for most people. It cannot be bent or manipulated to look like other 'responsible, real-world, capitalist work'. If you try, you will exhaust yourself and lose your creative power, and the world will mourn all that you had to create but couldn't, because you tried to make painting resemble something that might happen in a fluorescent-lit office in a high-rise.

If you choose to be an artist, your life will not look like anyone else's. And that is hard. And that is beautiful.

Don't fight it. If you do, you'll burn out.

CREATIVES DON'T UNDERSTAND THAT ART IS TIRING

We've been taught that art is a rest activity, a play activity. We're told that art should always be replenishing. (And it can be!) We tell schoolkids to do art when they're done with their *real* work. It's what we're finally allowed to do when we retire – a reward for doing the *real* job. Art is the dessert, after we've eaten all the vegetables.

But this rigid social categorisation has led us to gaslight ourselves when art makes us tired. It has stopped artists from resting properly and respecting their work as 'real' work. I'm experiencing this phenomenon writing this book. I crashed hard this weekend, absolutely wiped after a week of writing. 'What's wrong with me?' I said to James, who gently explained to me that I was trying to write a sixty-thousand-word book in two months and that might take a little bit of effort.

It can be hard to understand that the thing we love to do is also draining. I personally don't even notice how much energy it takes to write. I am absorbed. Focused. When I fall apart on the weekend, I cannot comprehend how this has happened! For a long time, the tiredness didn't make sense to me, so I ignored my body giving me clues, because I didn't think she had a valid reason for being tired. *You just wrote a story about a wizard all week, you loser, how could you be tired? Oliver, our dear doctor friend, has been saving lives! He's allowed to sleep.* There is lots to unpack in this narrative. I was not valuing art as a life-changing and powerful thing. I was not respecting it as a legitimate form of work, and I was ignoring every single sign my body was giving me.

Art is a form of work. It takes energy. You need to take breaks from it.

CREATING TAKES ENERGY. ART CAN BE EXHAUSTING. REST.

OTHER REASONS WE BURN OUT

I could write an anthology about the different ways creatives burn out. The ones above are those I see most often, but below I've composed a list of other ways you are vulnerable to exhausting yourself.

I want you to look for yourself in this list. Pay close attention to patterns you may be currently engaging in. We must stay vigilant for these energy leaks.

- You want your creations to be seen, for your art to connect. So you push and push against systems that are not here to serve you (e.g., gatekeepers, who only accept 'the best' but are essentially random and often biased).
- You hide behind perfectionism and so never let yourself finish your projects. You constantly try to improve your work but never deem yourself good enough.
- You buy into the story that only the very few 'make it', and in order to be the very few, you must work harder than the rest.
- You procrastinate, and procrastination is exhausting.
- You jump from creative project to creative project, never finishing, because they are never 'good enough'. You never enjoy the reward of seeing your art finished, or your art connecting to others.
- You are chronically ill or disabled and try to 'keep up' with everyone else, when your energy levels or your physical experience does not allow for that.
- You are part of a minority that has been systemically discriminated against, and so you feel the need to prove your worth by working harder than anyone else.
- You are creating while constantly feeling like a fraud and impostor, never truly embodying your role as creator, constantly fighting with yourself over whether you deserve to be doing what you are doing, which I can assure you will screw you right up and make you tired to your core.

- You are trying to balance art with your noncreative life. Leading these two lives – balancing them, managing them both – can be incredibly exhausting.
- You have found that one thing you are good at and that connects with others, and so you continue to create this one thing over and over again, getting no creative variance and wearing yourself down.
- You create only for external validation.

I've spent a lot of time looking at all the different reasons why artists burn out. I've done so because if you don't understand why you become exhausted, you get stuck in cycles.

It's okay if you find yourself exhausted and run-down. It's very valid. It's very reasonable. It's very real. Now we are going to look at how we prevent and recover from creative burnout.

HOW DO WE PREVENT BURNOUT?

For most of us, preventing burnout is an active practice. I don't think we can close our eyes, live a creative life and simply pray for the best. As I've just shown, there are too many ways you can accidentally, unconsciously push yourself too far. For creatives, art is a discipline, and rest must be a discipline. I want to talk now about some of the tools we can use to prevent burnout.

ADOPT BARE MAXIMUMS

Some of us are natural resters. If this is you, you are incredible. You've probably been told you're lazy. But you're not. You're skilled. You've kept up a practice that the world has desperately tried to stamp out of you in favour of productivity.

However, some of us (me) have (understandably) succumbed to the inundation of narratives about busyness and hustle. I find rest to be the most

You don't need to keep up momentum, stay in the algorithm's favour, race to remain relevant, battle with stagnancy. Trust the rhythm of your creative journey. Stillness is not stagnancy. You are always evolving. You are momentum.

unnatural thing to do and I must make it a discipline, just as I make writing a discipline. Cards on the table: I still suck.

If you struggle to rest like me, I recommend instituting a bare maximum. You know about bare minimums, the tiny, embarrassing amount of art I like you to do regularly. I touched on maximums in the reset too. The purpose of the maximum in the reset is to make it easy for you to stick to the program and prevent overworking. The bare maximum is a brilliant tool for artists who are obsessed with productivity and are therefore prone to overreach and burnout. If you've internalised hustle culture's push for ultimate output (and sadly most of us have), you will need to put measures in place to protect yourself from those narratives. You'll need a bare maximum. An upper limit.

I learned this from Greg McKeown, author of *Essentialism* and *Effortless*, two great books for chronic overworkers. The optimal amount of work for you to do in a day is usually quite a bit less than you are capable of doing if you went all out. Less in the short term means more in the long term. There's no point in working to 100 per cent of your capacity every day for six months if it means you burn out and can't even work to 10 per cent for the next six months.

For this book, I am on a tight deadline, so I have a large (for me) bare minimum of one thousand words a day, double what I normally do. I've decided to set a maximum word count per day of fifteen hundred. I know I could do more. If I went all out, I could probably do a lot more. But that would put me at risk of completely burning out after a few weeks, at which point I'd be stuck with a very quickly derived forty thousand words and no energy for the remaining twenty thousand. If I ignore my bare maximum, the consequences aren't good. This was reinforced recently when I cried for two days straight and couldn't figure out why. Turns out I had exceeded my maximum for a few days beforehand. I essentially lost two days of writing because I had decided to ignore my upper limit. If I had done it for a few more days, who knows? I might have missed my deadline, and been miserable, all for the sake of a couple of days of 'winning' the productivity war.

Most of us don't even think of capping how much we work. We have been taught that more is best. Output is the highest priority. It is not. Artists should be obsessed with sustainability. We want long, delightful, creative lives. We must work in a way that allows for that. Having a maximum level of work for the day prevents us from getting carried away. It is a gift for the artist we will be tomorrow.

Because of the ever-present productivity stories that knit the capitalist world together, a lot of you (and me!) have fallen out of touch with your bodies' signals. You don't even know when you need to stop or rest. You've spent years ignoring the signals to slow down, and now you just blow past them, leaving you terribly confused and surprised when you burn out! How did this happen? Maximums allow for us to protect ourselves, even when we are not so good at listening to our body's signals.

FIND YOUR HOLY PACE

Say you listen to some podcast and discover that Brandon Sanderson, perhaps the most prolific fantasy author of the past decade, aims for two thousand words a day. This is incredibly inspiring. You look at how many books he has out (over fifty at the time of this writing) and imagine how amazing it would feel to have written fifty books. You ignore the next part of the interview, where Sanderson says he doesn't recommend that early career writers write much more than five hundred words a day. Instead, you see a huge goal and run toward it. Then, after three days of trying to write like literally the most prolific writer we have ever heard of, you find the juice is gone. Because of course it is.

Trying to mimic successful artists – and completely and utterly ignoring your own rhythms, routines, energy levels and sleep needs – is a recipe for burnout. You think that their routine is what makes them successful. But it isn't the routine itself. It's the fact that the routine works for them.

You will have to find your own routine. You do this by simply paying attention to what feels good, what works, what absolutely doesn't work as you create. And after you've noticed (this is the crucial part), respect the findings!

CREATOR, YOUR PACE IS HOLY.

Don't try making art at five in the morning, have it absolutely wreck you, but continue to do it because it worked for Toni Morrison. Respect your findings! Try a new experiment. Maybe you're a night owl? Or maybe you're a lunch break person. You are an entirely unique artist who needs an entirely unique, *bespoke* creative routine. Spend time figuring out what it could look like and what it absolutely does not look like and then honour it.

Your pace is holy.

Your pace is holy.

Your pace is holy.

Please rebel. Rebel against productivity culture. Rebel against Brandon Sanderson. Rebel against anything that doesn't serve you and your art. The most important part of all of this is your pace, your routines, what works for you. You are wasting your precious time trying to fit yourself into 'proven routines and schedules' when they most certainly haven't been proven to work for you.

I know it would be so much easier to just be told what to do. But that isn't the game we play when we create. Our routines, our pace, they are bespoke.

STOP TRYING TO PRETEND YOU ARE A NORMAL, REGULAR PERSON

If we commit to our art, we are breaking some fairly foundational social rules, namely, do something safe, do something normal, produce something 'practical', have something boring to tell people at parties or family gatherings. Going against the status quo is tiring.

I spent the first five years of being a writer at war with myself. Fifty per cent of me was like, *I am going to be an author! I don't care what the world thinks of that!* And the other 50 per cent was like, *You are a loser, and everyone thinks you're deluded. Get back in line.*

This internal war was exhausting. I was never at peace. Leaning into the archetype of the rebel helped bring my internal world to peace.

Artist, you are not meant to fit in. Trying to fit in will exhaust you.

Artist, your work life will not look like the traditional work life. Trying to make it look 'normal' will exhaust you.

Artist, your priorities won't look like their priorities. That is good. That is magic.

Lean into being a bit weird. Fighting it is going to exhaust you. Break the rules. Don't do what they expect you to do. You are an artist. You are not here to conform or stay small. Fighting your natural instinct to create leads to burnout. Embrace it, exhale, you are doing so well.

ALLOW IT TO BE EASY

We don't want to simply evade burnout. We want to invite ease into our creative lives. The dominant narrative is that creativity is hard. The legacy of the struggling artist myth is thriving.

I don't want you to inherit it.

Of course, as we've seen in this act of the book, there are real trials and difficulties that you encounter as an artist. I will always validate your pain, but I refuse to engage in the idea that art itself is pain. There is so much ease and flow available to you.

As previously mentioned, most of us don't want ease in our creative life, because making art and having it be easy would be morally wrong. We believe that meaningful things must be hard. So before looking at *how* we invite ease and flow into our journeys, we need to get comfortable with the idea that life is about to be really, really good. A lot of you won't be okay with that. Most of us are so used to the struggle that being without it feels deeply unsafe. Our brains go into withdrawal. Where is the stress hormone? Where is the depression and anxiety? Where is the pain?

This was a big hurdle in my journey to creative ease. I didn't believe I deserved it.

HERE IS MY DECLARATION TO YOU

You deserve to make your art joyfully. You deserve ease. You deserve to do what you want to do with your life. You are allowed to find things easy. Finding things easy is a beautiful and natural part of being an artist. You don't have to be struggling to be a worthy human being. You don't have to be tired and exhausted to deserve joy. You don't have to be busy to be a real adult. I know there are people in the world who are in pain, who are moving through monumental tragedy, and I know that when you sit with your watercolours with a smile on your face, it can feel unfair. Why do you deserve this when others don't have the time or opportunity?

If you are able to read this book, you have been given a chance to create art joyfully. Why? I don't know. But you have. You cannot martyr yourself, your joy, your art, in the name of those who do not have this opportunity. *That* is immoral and useless, and helps nobody. It is time to take up the mantle and lead the way, to be a delighted and joyful creative. You don't deserve creative abundance *more* than those who are deprived of it because of war, or profound poverty, or systemic oppression. We all deserve it. And you aren't going to waste this opportunity.

I need you to stop feeling guilt. Guilt haemorrhages energy. I need you to stop committing to the idea that art must be hard. I need you to be open to ease.

Creativity will never be 100 per cent smooth sailing, but we must realise that it can be much easier than you're making it. You can unclench your fists, loosen those shoulders, uncrinkle your brow. It isn't a moral requirement to grind through your art.

Here are some of the many ways you can invite ease into your creative practice, many of which we've discussed:

- Creating habits, thus taking away the constant need for motivation.
- Practising bare minimums, thus allowing us to show up easily, with low expectations of output.

- Practising bare maximums, thus protecting our energy so we don't go too hard.
- Allowing ourselves to make shitty art, thus relieving ourselves of the pressure of making good art while still showing up.
- Cultivating patience and trust, thus relieving the feeling of constantly pushing and waiting.
- Choosing yourself before you are chosen by others, so the power originates from you, not from depending on others.

So much of our pain comes from never being in flow – always being reactive. We don't want to be constantly making decisions, we don't want to be constantly trying, pushing ourselves through this creative journey with pure force of will. When you integrate this list into your creative journey, you make space, you are in control. You have the power. You invite in ease.

YOU MIGHT HAVE TO BURN OUT TO FIGURE OUT WHAT BURNS YOU OUT

Too often we must touch the flame to really *know* it's hot. That's okay; it's very human.

Besides, what burns you out will be different from what burns me out. You need to go on this journey yourself. I can't burn out for you. Maybe I'm talking to a burnout expert right now, with two dozen serious burnouts under your belt, and you're laughing at me for trying to teach you this stuff.

I see you. I want the most recent burnout to be your last.

YOU DID IT – YOU BURNT OUT

I'm so sorry this happened. We are so vulnerable to going too hard, and I don't want you to beat yourself up for reaching your end point. I also don't want you to glamorise burnout, something I have been known to do. When I burnt out, I used to get some sort of twisted pride that I worked so hard that I was medically ill. I did it, I reached the capitalist finish line. But as we've discussed, this capitalist finish line is a sick joke and stops artists from making cool shit.

We can't beat ourselves up, and we can't take pride in our exhaustion. What we need is radical self-compassion and acceptance. We also need to use this experience to learn. Burnout sucks but it provides information. We have been so detached from how it is we like to create, work, face ourselves, but now we know something. The way we were doing it wasn't sustainable. Pay attention to what exhausted you and what energises you. What was the last straw that led to this? What patterns were you in that weren't serving you? What pace were you going? Understand that it wasn't serving you.

I see a lot of creatives burn out, rest, recover, and then go do the same thing they were doing before. I did this because I couldn't understand why I couldn't do the routine I'd set for myself: *Loads of other people do way, way more than me and they're fine. It's embarrassing that I can't keep up with this comparatively small creative workload. I'm going to try again. Or, you know what, maybe I should go even harder than before* . . . It looks foolish when I lay it out like that, but we are so bad at getting to the root cause of things. We have been so convinced that we must define ourselves by our output that we can't accept that our standards are too high or that our capacity may not be what we think it should be.

I have a small capacity. Not just for art, but for everything. I'm one of those people who, if I have one thing going on in a day, can't have another thing going on. Even if it's a dentist appointment. I look at people who work long hours in offices, and I am literally in awe of their capacity. I look at actors who go from a matinee to an evening show and then repeat that schedule again and again for weeks, and I know I could never. We all have different capacities, and some of us have small capacities. We have been made to feel shame about this, but your pace is holy. Your rhythms are holy. Your capacity is holy. And you know what? Even as someone who likes to sleep for ten hours a day and who finds going to the dentist exhausting, I've still managed to write several books, build a business, grow an audience and finds lots of joy. I did this not by pushing through pain, but by discovering my limit and sticking to it.

SO HOW DO WE RECOVER?

Slowly. Even slower than what you're currently thinking. Also, there may be (and probably will be) false starts, when you go too hard and then you have to back up, rest again and try again. That's okay.

Recovery must start with rest. You've got to give up for a bit. You can't just be burnt out, realise it, and then dive back into your creative process. Most of the time, you're going to need time doing absolutely nothing. Let yourself miss it.

For those of you who don't know how to rest, I need a whole new book for you (and for me). The crux of it is that resting might be uncomfortable, but you're just going to have to deal with that. You will have to face the silence. You will have to listen to the voices inside your head. You might have to, God forbid, be bored. Rest doesn't come easy to a lot of us. It's never been demonstrated to us. That doesn't mean you get to avoid it. When we are exhausted, we need to stop.

STARTING SAFELY AGAIN

After rest, we recover with play. We need to take the pressures off our art and let ourselves get back to basics. That means mess. That means delight. That often means making art just for ourselves. It might mean trying a totally new craft, letting your creativity muscles work in a new realm entirely. Let yourself be a beginner again. See what that feels like. I'm currently writing in a café, and an elderly lady has ordered herself a cake and a coffee and is drawing; that seems like a good way to recover from burnout. Make it delightful. You might also like to recover by going back to the start of this book and doing the two-week reset. This whole book is, in essence, a guide to not burning out.

I want to leave this chapter with a message for those of you who are in the trenches:

You are still an artist when you've spent a long time away from your art.

You are still an artist when you're burnt out and resentful.

You are still an artist if you only do the tiniest amount of creating every now and again.

You are still an artist when you have a full-time muggle job that is taking up most of your life.

Don't let anyone take the title of Artist away from you. It is yours. And if you feel overwhelmed and scared right now, if you're so tired you can't even look at your paintbrush or your pen or think about being onstage, you are still an artist. It's okay. You can just be.

BURNOUT PROMPTS

If you are currently burnt out or exhausted, be extra careful with these prompts. Take them slowly. Write a sentence here, then come back to it later. Record it as a voice note, or just spend time thinking about the questions. Do it at your pace, on your own terms.

1. **What are your warning signs that you're tired?** This prompt is here to encourage you to reconnect with your body and mind. We are done with ignoring the signals. We need to know when we need to slow down and take care of ourselves. I want you to look at this question from two perspectives: your physical signs of exhaustion (e.g., a tight feeling across your chest, extra yawning) and your mental signs of exhaustion (e.g., you're easily distractable, everything feels hard, very little flow, unwelcome narratives such as *You're so lazy*, etc.).

2. **What draws energy out? What brings energy in?** Become aware of what's robbing you of energy and what fills you up. The more you

become conscious of what drains you and what elevates you, the more you can course correct when you feel tired. You'll have a whole list of activities and moments that refuel you!

3. **Describe a sustainable creative practice for yourself. What are you doing? What aren't you doing? What pace do you create at? How often do you rest?** This protocol might feel idealistic and unobtainable right now, but it's important to consider what a sustainable and energy-filled art practice looks like for you. You might also feel embarrassed or ashamed about how slow you need to work in order for it to be sustainable, but this is conditioning from a culture obsessed with the hustle. Be gentle with yourself.

ACT FOUR

BUILDING AN ABUNDANT PRACTICE

We've made a case for creativity, we've taken up the mantle of Artist and we have faced resistance.

Now for the fun part.

In this act of the book, we will look at developing, enhancing and finessing your practice. What will your creative legacy be? What sort of art are you going to leave behind? How will you use your voice? How will you use failure? How will you handle your creative success?

I want you to be a thriving artist. You aren't here to spend your whole life fighting resistance. You're here for abundance and for excellence. Let's make it happen.

YOU: THERE'S TOO MUCH NOISE! THERE'S NO SPACE FOR ME!

ME: THERE'S NO NOISE LIKE YOUR NOISE. WE NEED YOUR VOICE.

ON VOICE

To begin this act, we start with your voice. Whether you sing, sew, design games or make puppets, you have a distinct creative voice that you can develop, hone, change, finesse. We need your voice. We need your very unique way of making things. So, in this chapter, we will look at who you are as an artist. We will discover the nuances and magic of your own expression. How do you develop your voice? What even *is* voice? How do you avoid the many pitfalls of trying to be different? What are you going to say?

WHAT DO I MEAN WHEN I SAY *YOUR VOICE*?

When I speak about voice, I am talking about your creative style, flair, essence. For a writer, it's our language, our tone, our way with words. I am a very 'voicey' writer. I have my idiosyncrasies and quirks. Some writers try to eradicate voice, preferring to have blander, more prosaic writing, not wanting to distract the reader from the content or story. But even if you are trying to get back to basics, no one can truly avoid having a creative voice. You have your ways; they are immutable.

In crafts other than writing, the voice comes through in a plethora of ways. The way you photograph landscapes with a certain type of focus, the intentional rigidity of the way you move when you dance, the way you use your eyebrows when you act, the undeniable romance of your paintings. It is a hard concept to articulate, but our creative voice is our individuality seeping through to our art. It's you, in art form.

THE OBSESSION WITH INNOVATION

When artists talk about developing their creative voice, it quickly becomes a conversation about how to be innovative and how to make something that no one has seen before. This makes sense. You want your art to be different. But an obsession with innovation can get in your way. Too many artists feel that in order to be consequential they need to do something entirely new. This insistence on breaking the mould will keep you from your best work. Innovation isn't what makes you connect with your art, vulnerability is. So, as we begin a conversation about how you can express yourself and find your voice, I want to start with this: you are innately and effortlessly unique, and *trying* to be different is counterproductive. Creatives spend years and years trying to figure out what they could make that has never been made before when we don't need originality, we just need your vulnerable, generous art. I have seen too many important projects scrapped because they've 'been done before'. I have seen artists betray their own divine creative compass in the name of innovation. The obsession with innovation is distracting us from our own magic.

Every time you create, you will have a chance to play with your voice, but if you are obsessed with making something that has never been seen before, you will be so preoccupied with that impossible task that you'll lose sight of your own potential.

And I am so sorry, but true innovation *is* a near impossible task. Your idea, your concept, your notion will have, in some way, been done before. And I know this sounds like terrible news, but it really isn't anything of the sort. Art isn't the search for originality. Innovation isn't the purpose of artistry. Vulnerability is.

A LOT OF ARTISTS ARE ADDICTED TO INNOVATION AND FEEL THAT THEIR CREATIONS WILL BE CONSEQUENTIAL ONLY IF THEY ARE ENTIRELY NEW. THIS BELIEF WILL KEEP YOU FROM YOUR BEST WORK. INNOVATION ISN'T WHAT MAKES PEOPLE CONNECT TO YOUR ART. VULNERABILITY IS.

WHAT THE HECK DO I MEAN BY *VULNERABLE ART?*

Vulnerable art is art that is inextricably linked with you. Brené Brown defines vulnerability as emotional exposure. Vulnerable art makes you feel emotionally exposed. You've put a part of yourself into your creation and you feel revealed. When I ask you to stop making innovative art and start making vulnerable art, I am asking you to stop trying to make something new and start making something you. Your worldview, your emotions, your pain, your joy, your relationships, your noticings, your culture, your heritage, your ancestry, your fears, your desires, your trauma, your love. Your truth.

When you make vulnerable art, you make something that is true. If you choose to share it, people will see their own truth in it. If you choose to share it, people will have a little bit of you in their homes. This is the art I am trying to make. The art that makes me squirm with the thought of people seeing me like this. The art that feels like I am having the most personal conversation with the world. The art made without my defences up. The art that says I am human and I made something, witness me.

So what's the difference between being unique and making something entirely new? It's a tricky difference to articulate, but I think the biggest difference between being innovative and being unique is that being unique takes no effort at all. While the world may have seen ideas like yours many times before, you have an entirely unique lens through which to filter your ideas. You are a onetime phenomenon in the universe. You have never been seen before and you will never be seen again. Connecting to yourself, the way you see the world, the way you move – these things lead to unique art. Effortlessly. Not innovative art. Unique art. It is yours, and while it might have been seen in some shape or form before, it's never been seen in this specific way.

Take, for example, the many world-changing books on the creative process out there. I've read them. They've healed me. I have agreed with them. I have disagreed with them. Now it's my turn to speak on this subject. I am not actively trying to be different from the lineage of books on creativity. Like Elizabeth Gilbert in *Big Magic*, I am trying to be as vulnerable as possible, as true

INSTEAD OF CREATING VIRAL ART, CREATE VULNERABLE ART.

as possible, as generous as possible as I alchemise my ideas onto the page. Like Julia Cameron, I want to take gentle care of the artist and give you permission to chase your creative dreams.

But unlike these two creative godmothers, I am deep in the trenches of my creative career. I am speaking on this topic from my unique circumstance, which happens to be earlier in my career as an author and artist. I am still rejected frequently. I know the pain of trying to establish myself as an artist very well. I remember what it feels like to have no one want your art, and what it's like to make art with no deadlines, because I am still doing it today! I have built my career as someone who speaks to artists as a peer. As someone for whom the continual distractions, roadblocks and course corrections are part of my every day.

I am writing a book that overlaps with many of the topics Rick Rubin wrote about in his masterpiece *The Creative Act*, but I am not Rick Rubin looking back on a recording session with the Red Hot Chili Peppers. I am Amie, someone who is intimately familiar with the pains and problems of the beginner and the intermediate. Who coaches thousands of clients who worry more about starting at all than finessing the final track of their certain-to-be-multiplatinum album. My advice is practical, it is grounded, it is steeped in the everyday mess and problems of the journeyman. Of the side project. Of the part-time hustler, and the multi-job juggler, and the mum writing for five minutes after putting the kids to bed, and the college student whose tutor just told them they'll never make it. These are the problems I'm interested in.

We must learn to trust our own voice, our own unique perspective, our own brand of magic. Come home and realise you are effortlessly unique; you don't need to be overtly innovative.

'But', you say, 'the saturated market! How will I stand out! There are so many people out there making stuff! Social media is so loud! There is too much noise! There are too many creative people!'

Remember: Art is not toaster. Humans have an insatiable appetite for art. We do not get full. I watched *Everything Everywhere All at Once* last week. Do you think I'm not interested in high-concept sci-fi anymore? No! If I could have a hundred movies like that, I would watch every single one of them. My curiosity and lust for words, stories, ideas aren't capped. I don't need art to be ENTIRELY DIFFERENT in order for it to connect with me. Innovation isn't the key for connection.

Again, vulnerable, true, personal art is.

DEVELOPING YOUR VOICE BY USING THE VOICES OF OTHERS

Whether you are doing it consciously or not, you will use other artists as a way of defining your own voice. We are influenced by other pieces of art. And that's good. It's beautiful. We are not here to create in a vacuum. Austin Kleon, in his book *Steal Like an Artist*, suggests that we are part of a lineage of artists, we are the apprentices of our artist ancestors. We get to learn and take from the masters, whether we know them personally or not.

I simply cannot read a Terry Pratchett book without then inflicting his tone of voice upon characters in my own novels. In fact, I know Sir Terry has been an important part of defining the voice I use when I write fiction. His playful, silly humour has influenced me. I have used it and learned from it. I am not a Terry Pratchett fanfic writer. I am not copying his worlds or words. Rather, I have learned from his craft, and those brilliant lessons shimmer somewhere beneath my prose. Similarly, it would be unfair to detach Tolkien from anything I write, because his books and the movies based on them sat at the foundation of all my childhood imaginings.

Use art that you love to inform your own creative voice. Study it. Try imitating it. See what strange quirks happen when you use it as inspiration. Could you take those quirks further? Or did they not work at all? Take a facet, invert it, play with it. Get curious about how you can learn from their style.

This tactic might not feel aligned with you. And that's okay. As I mentioned in the comparison chapter, I know many creatives who intentionally fast, deliberately not consuming art when they are in the middle of a project. I know others who are afraid of comparing their work to that by artists they love, and so choose to stay away from this method. But I believe that whether you use this as an intentional exercise or not, it will happen. We are a Creative Congregation, we are in communion, and ideas are contagious.

I HAVE NOT BEEN TALKING ABOUT PLAGIARISM

I speak to so many artists who have navigated heartbreaking experiences of people stealing their work. I have too – from Oscar winners using my uncredited work to celebrate their wins, to some of the biggest names in music using my work to launch products, to random men on the internet taking my words, saying they're their own, and growing a following with them. These people didn't use my art to develop their own voice and style. They just took my work without credit.

I want to be very clear that when I talk about studying other artists' creations, I don't mean plagiarism. I am not talking about stealing someone else's art or ideas and passing them off as our own.

Instead, I am speaking to the process of learning from, being inspired by and being taught by artists we love.

COPYING OTHERS AS A WAY TO PROTECT FROM VULNERABILITY

We must be honest with ourselves about how we use other creatives' work. Are you copying Banksy because you want to find your voice through their style? Or are you copying Banksy because their style has already been externally validated, and if you just do what they did, then how could you screw up? You have too much to give to hide behind the style of other artists forever. Eventually you will have to step out of their shadows and find your own voice.

A similar thing happens in the world of social media. The obsession with going viral, or following trends, can distract us from what we want to make, from who we actually are as artists. We want to jump on a trend because we've seen someone else get huge views or interactions from it. I believe there is a place for using trends to develop our own voice, but we have to be careful. Too often, chasing what is currently making waves is a way of numbing and suppressing what we actually want to do. It is safer to replicate, to see what's doing well and produce that, than to dare to do what you want to do. It's a nuanced balancing act. Short-term engagement isn't really worth it if you aren't finding your own voice along the way. No one will stick around if all you do is recycle other people's art. They want to see something of you in it. It's easy to be swept away by what's trending and what's popular. So pay close attention to how you feel during the creative process and when you share the art. Actively ask yourself, *Is this something I want to create? Or is it something I feel I should create? Does this creative process feel good? Or does it feel cheap and misaligned?* Get to know your creative taste, appetite, voice.

SCREW THE NICHE

Another rumour that circulates in the creative community is that you need to find your niche and focus intently on one thing to get good and develop your style. The more you focus on that one art form, the better at it you'll get and the more you'll develop your voice.

I don't buy it.

We have been obsessed with specialisation for far too long, and while it might work for a lawyer or an accountant, I am going to argue that art doesn't thrive under specialisation. Creativity supports creativity. It's stunningly symbiotic. We don't have to limit our expression to one form of it.

In his book *Range*, David Epstein counteracts the myth of intense specialisation that Malcolm Gladwell popularised in the mega-bestselling *Outliers*. Epstein argues that there might be some tasks that lend themselves to lifelong specialisation, but these are usually simple, closed-system activities where we can get immediate feedback on whether we've succeeded at what we're trying to do, and where the variables rarely change. Golf is a good example. It's just you and the ball. As soon as you make things more complex, like in tennis where you add just one more player actively working to thwart you, suddenly specialisation isn't as important. Suddenly, the player who tried a few different sports when they were younger has an edge because they're able to incorporate the skills they've learned from other disciplines to the court. Similarly in art, you may be able to get very good at playing an instrument if you specialise, but things that are less objective, like writing music, improvising, adding style and flair, require a broad range of skills.

My voice as a writer can be developed in my work as a painter because finding my voice as an artist is about finding my voice as a person. I can become a better writer on a long walk on a summer's evening. I can improve as an artist in the supermarket, staring absentmindedly at the gluten-free section, or on a long car trip as I talk out loud to myself in a fake interview. I can grow and expand as a creative anywhere if I am paying attention.

There are too many artists painfully letting go of creative or even noncreative hobbies in the name of improvement through specialisation. Your art practice is always. If you want, your entire life can be a devotion to your creative practice. There is no time wasted. Please let yourself be a fully expansive and expressive human being, with multiple creative outlets. Please know that they all inform each other, and the weird way you knit jumpers can be translated into the weird way you take photos. Your voice is your essence, and it will spill into everything you do.

WE CAN DEVELOP OUR VOICE AND STYLE AT ANY MOMENT OF THE DAY

As I noted earlier, we can become better and better artists everywhere and all the time. Isn't that just the best? It delights me.

Notice things. Know yourself. Daydream. Play. Have interesting conversations. Keep a notes file on your phone. Pay attention. Move slowly, with intention. All of this is in service to your art, to your voice. Stop thinking art must be a deeply serious, painful slog. Artists are meant to have lots of interests. We're meant to have full and random and interesting lives. We are not meant to lock ourselves in dark rooms and bleed.

Of course, we must eventually translate these experiences into the art itself. The best way to deepen your connection to your style is, to be blunt, by making art. The more you can play with your craft, the more you can figure out what works and what doesn't. The more you can push the boat out and embarrass yourself a little, the more you will understand what you want to do and how you want to do it. If we are brave enough to try new and potentially embarrassing things, we will discover the things that delight us.

The key is, though, you have to be willing to go there. You have to be willing to look at what you've done and feel a little embarrassed. You have to be imperfect, you have to be raw, otherwise you will tiptoe around greatness your whole life. You will spend your time swimming in the shallows because the depths look dark and scary, when, in reality, they are where the hidden treasure lies.

Art is the gateway to knowing yourself. So let the creative process reveal all your intrinsic, bizarre, beautiful, varied and idiosyncratic ways. Enjoy this process of honing your style and playing with expression. Finding your voice and experimenting with the way you create is a form of play. So get messy, and have fun.

VOICE PROMPTS

Journalling is a beautiful way to develop your voice. The more you know yourself, the stronger your creative voice will get. These prompts are specifically designed as an exercise to develop your unique creative style.

1. **How do you use the practice of imitation?** Do you copy or borrow from other people's art? Do you resist it because it feels like cheating? Do you hide behind it because you're afraid to make something that is wholly yours or that reveals something about yourself? Investigate your relationship with learning from those who have come before you.

2. **Have you been limiting your creative practice in the name of niching down?** In your ideal world, how widespread would your creative practice be? Follow any curiosity. Invite in any desire. Think maybe you'd quite like acting but have never tried it? Write it down.

3. **How would you describe your creative voice?** Be an art critic, a book reviewer, a fan, a patron. Or perhaps pretend you're listening to an interview on your favourite podcast or show about your art. What are these people saying? Whatever the setting, describe your creative voice. Notice how it feels to discuss your flair and style. Be idealistic. Be wanky about it. You might not be at the stage you want to be right now, that's okay, write as if you're already there. Sink into who you are becoming. Focus on the things you do better than other people. The things that make your work pop.

NOTHING TRULY WONDERFUL IS MADE WITHOUT FIRST BEING A LITTLE BIT CRINGE.

ON SELF-CENSORSHIP

This chapter follows on from the voice chapter seamlessly because we cannot hone our creative voice if we are in a practice of self-censorship. Africa Brooke, author of *The Third Perspective*, defines self-censorship as 'when you silence your own voice and hold back thoughts, feelings, or knowledge out of fear, doubt, or the desire to fit in'. Self-censorship squashes creativity. We cannot thrive in the habit of it, yet so many of us are.

Artists will betray their vision and contort themselves into all sorts of shapes in order to be palatable and safe. You sacrifice your brilliance, your vulnerability, your message in the name of pleasing everyone. You water down your art so you don't rock the boat.

Once you have developed a reliable and unique practice, once you begin discovering your voice and style, you cannot start diluting yourself in order to be consumable. You can't self-censor.

In this chapter, we will discuss three sorts of self-censorship. First, we'll talk about people-pleasing and the problems that arise when you want your art to be infallible and liked by everyone. Next, we will look at artists who desperately don't want to embarrass themselves. And finally, we're going to look at the fear that the digital age has caused.

You can't come all this way, fight all your perfectionist, procrastinating demons, carve out time in your life to create, and then make art that is penitent and censored. Your artistic vision cannot be sacrificed to your own self-censorship.

SELF-CENSORING THROUGH PEOPLE-PLEASING

Dedicating time to creativity can feel indulgent and frivolous. To atone for daring to do something so silly, you might make art that is apologetic. You make art that you hope will please everyone. You make art that couldn't possibly offend or be distasteful. Everyone could like this piece you are currently working on; it's a universal piece of art! For the masses. But in striving for the world to like you, you guarantee no one will *love* you.

You betray yourself (and your audience) when you go down the people-pleasing road. Some of us practise this overtly, knowingly censoring ourselves. You say no to ideas and concepts you feel called to explore because you know it won't vibe with certain people. You picture your bemused grandmother, the angry politician, the snobbish critic, and think, *Let's dial it back.* For many of us, it is a single person who triggers people-pleasing art. That art teacher who punished you when you tried something different, or a parent who laughed at you when you described the political factions and the unique magic of the fantasy world you were working on. Other creatives go on an unconscious people-pleasing journey. Slowly and unknowingly you water down your creativity. You've practised 'not being too much' your entire life, so toning down your self-expression comes naturally to you.

However we do it, nearly all of us, at some point, will get stuck making art to please.

WHAT'S SO BAD ABOUT ART THAT PLEASES?

There is absolutely nothing wrong with wanting to make art that connects. That makes impact. That delights people! Creatives are often told that they must make art only for themselves. I don't believe in that. I don't believe the

PEOPLE PLEASERS WILL ALWAYS STRUGGLE TO MAKE ART BECAUSE ART WILL ALWAYS RUFFLE FEATHERS AND NEVER BE TO EVERYONE'S TASTE.

ON SELF-CENSORSHIP

audience has to come last. I make art that brings me joy, but I am not creating it just for me. I want others to enjoy it too.

I think about my reader when I write – it is, in essence, a collaboration between my reader and me. For example, my latest novel is about a sixteenth-century urchin detective who solves crime on the streets of Tudor London. I know, through reviews and feedback, that my readers loved the cosy cottagecore that I had in my last book. So I'm popping my rapscallion of an investigator in a cute little tavern. I didn't betray my own creative vision by inserting an adorable, possibly historically inaccurate pub into my book. I thought about what my audience might want, and I agreed with them, even though that wasn't necessarily in the original scope of the story. The audience doesn't come last when I create art.

If you are a creator who wants to connect to others with your art, I need you to feel free to daydream about your reader/patron/customer/viewer/audience. It is not selfish or indulgent to want an audience or want to connect. It does not dishonour your art to think about the consumer. It doesn't tarnish the purity of your process to consider how it will be received. Art isn't a pure thing anyhow; it is messy and human and ridiculous. Please strategise, consider and fall in love with those who will consume and enjoy your art. Be in communion with them.

The problem arises, and your art is affected, when you give your audience or imagined audience too much say. There must be balance. You must remain in power.

You must remember that you are the artist. No one else can be in charge of your creative choices. You get the final say. If you are *constantly* thinking about what others think, and the core focus of your creativity is on their opinion, you will make art that is painfully mediocre and bland. A piece of art isn't something that everyone should like. There is nothing in the world that everyone agrees is great. And if I'm wrong, and something universally beloved does exist, it is definitely not art.

Art is here to divide. Which means, Artist, you are here to divide.

PEOPLE-PLEASING CREATIVES WILL ALWAYS STRUGGLE

People-pleasing doesn't affect only the quality of your art. It also affects *how* you create, it affects how you talk about your art, it affects how you market your art, and it affects how you put boundaries around your art. For the people-pleasing creative, every step of your journey is going to be in the name of regulating someone else's emotions. That will exhaust you. I have collated a list below of the ways people-pleasing can affect your creative journey. I want you to read it carefully. A lot of us are so used to accommodating others that we don't realise we are people-pleasing artists.

Some signs you're a people-pleasing creative:

- You feel uncomfortable and guilty for wanting to be a creative because asking for and chasing what you want feels selfish.
- You don't ask for support because you don't want to inconvenience or burden anyone.
- You don't make the art you really want to make because you're afraid it will 'ruffle feathers' or upset someone.
- You can't stop thinking about what your mum will say if she sees it. (Sometimes people-pleasing artists have a specific focus on one or a few specific individuals who they worry will hate it, creating only with that specific lens.)
- You feel responsible for people's reactions toward you and your art, so you spend endless amounts of energy curating and trying to control their responses.
- You make art that has a very hard-to-define audience, and you spend an awful lot of time trying to make sure that your creations relate and connect to everyone. Heaven forbid the boys down at the golf club don't want to read my sixteenth-century romance novel!
- You feel really tired after creating because you've viewed your art through your entire high school class's lens the whole time.

- You create only when no one else 'needs you'. You never want your art to inconvenience anyone, so you rarely do it.

People-pleasing Creative, there are consequences to your actions. You're not going to get the support you need, you're going to water down your art, you're going to deny your audience the chance to witness you, you're going to sacrifice your creating time for others. Being a people-pleasing creative doesn't mean you try to make art that delights people, it means you sacrifice your vision, your potential, your magic.

WHY IS IT ON YOUR SHOULDERS TO MAKE ART FOR EVERYONE?

Why aren't you allowed to make what delights you? Was this a story that was taught to you when you were young? Were you responsible for the equilibrium in your home as a child? And now you're responsible for the equilibrium of the world? You must ask yourself these hard questions.

From childhood, many of you will have been taught to not rock the boat, to not ruffle feathers. Children are told to stay quiet. In school, you write the essay the teachers want. When we grow old, there are similar expectations. Do what the boss wants, make sure you're posting the 'right things' on social media. But the artist needs to be loud, they need to make whatever they are called to make, they must not contain themselves; they must let their emotions fly. It is on you to take care of your inner child, your inner artist, and reparent them.

I'm someone who has a tendency to believe she is responsible for the well-being of everyone around her at all times. It's something I'm working through, and it's taking a long time. These are big narratives to rewrite. I've been taught since I was little that I'm safest when everyone around me is emotionally regulated, so I spend a lot of time being very concerned about everyone's feelings. Just today, when my partner, James, asked me what the weather was going to be like, I checked the app, saw it was going to rain, clocked that James really needed to catch some sunshine (it's his first English winter), and then proceeded to mildly lie to him about how the weather would unfold. 'Sure, it's raining now, but I think it's going to clear up! There's going to be sun' (at 1:00 p.m. it would stop raining for an hour). I did this entirely unconsciously. I had a neural pathway that fired: I needed James to be okay, and so I lied about the weather. If I pull this crap on my husband, you bet I am pulling this crap when I write my novels. What sacrifices am I making to ensure my readers are 'happy'? I must be so careful about the intentions behind my choices. I must ask myself the question: Am I writing this story because it's true and vulnerable? Or am I trying to get my mum to feel good about how she raised me? If we don't recognise these patterns, we're destined to create watered-down art.

The story about my lying to James about the weather is a good example of how people-pleasing isn't actually about pleasing people. It's about keeping ourselves safe. When I lied about the sun coming out, that was about me, not James. When you try to make art that will make everyone happy, you aren't being generous, you're trying to protect yourself from harm. And you don't need to be upset with yourself about that, but you do need to understand it.

People-pleasing is how you protect yourself, and it's a way of manipulating those around you so that you feel safe. It's not a sustainable or abundant place to create art from.

PEOPLE-PLEASING CAN GET WAY, WAY WORSE WITH SUCCESS

You might think the urge to please people goes away with traditional success. That if you won a Grammy, you'd finally feel confident enough to truly be the artist you want to be. Unfortunately, this crap never ends unless you choose to put a stop to it. It is not just an affliction of the beginner; it can get worse the more successful you get. In fact, I see far more traditionally successful artists immobilised by people-pleasing tendencies than I do new artists. This phenomenon has been dubbed audience capture. You find a little bit of success and then double down on whatever caused that success.

Say you write a blog post about bees and it goes viral. You aren't even that interested in bees. In fact, you usually write about slugs. But bees seemed to strike a nerve. So you start tailoring all your content to be about bees, and suddenly all you've done for ten years is produce an endless torrent of bee content!

Creatives find their audience and then believe they owe those audiences everything, or that the audience will turn their backs on them if they don't produce more of the same. The second book in a series, the role in the boring movie you hate, the album that riffs on the last one. They *have* to please the fans. They owe it to them.

This narrative will mess you right up. You don't owe your audience anything. You already gave them the art that they fell in love with. You can be grateful for your audience. What a pleasure to create for people who delight in your work! But you don't owe them anything. You are not working for them.

Creatives who create the same thing over and over and over again in the name of pleasing their audience are working from fear. This sort of people-pleasing comes from a scarcity story you've been fed about artists. 'Only the very lucky find an audience'. You believe that if you are lucky enough to find an audience, you must hold on to your patrons with all your might! What if they leave you? But you stagnate when you follow this train of thought. You halt your creative evolution. You are actually betraying your audience by giving them something watered down.

HOW DO I LEARN TO DISAPPOINT PEOPLE?

Undoing these stories can take time. But there are things you can do to ease you into the true and important naughtiness of being a creative. As you learn to take up space unapologetically, you need methods with built-in safety nets. You will have to do scary things, but you also deserve a sense of safety as you do them. I'm going to detail a few tactics that I've seen work for recovering people pleasers:

CREATE A SECRET OR ANONYMOUS SPACE TO SHARE ART

One of the most powerful and simple things I did on my creative journey was start a new and secret Instagram profile. I blocked everyone I knew. It took hours. The randoms from high school and the old colleagues who didn't even know my last name – everyone I knew was blocked. I wanted space to subvert expectations. I wanted space to disappoint. I wanted space to be cringe. And I needed to have eyes off me as I leaned into this. That secret Instagram page is now, of course, the platform on which I have built my writing career. But I didn't start it to grow my profile as a writer. I started it as a love letter to myself and artists like me. To give creative people like me a place to take themselves seriously.

This is also why pen names can be amazing. One of my writing friends has not one but two pseudonyms. One is for their traditionally published work and another is for self-pubbed, which is much darker than their traditionally published work. When I've asked them why they segment themselves like that, their answer is that the first pen name protects them from friends and family, the second from their audience.

When I suggest people make a secret profile, or block everyone on social media, I get pushback. *It's cowardly! Let people just see you in all your majesty.* And look, it would be great if I had been brave enough to do that, but I wasn't. I never would have shared my writing if everyone could see it. I needed to start in a smaller, 'less brave' way. Give yourself the concessions you need. You don't have to go all in, all at once. Start small. See what grows from there.

LOOK AT BAD REVIEWS OF YOUR FAVOURITE CREATIONS

Incredible art is shitty in some people's eyes. I like to get closer to this truth by looking at the worst reviews for my favourite pieces of art. Look up your favourite movie, your favourite book, your favourite painting – *there will be critics*. Something you think is unassailable will have a litany of one-star reviews that look completely unhinged to your eyes. Print them off, put them in your office or your studio, or maybe next to your bed so you can integrate them while you dream. Your artistic heroes couldn't please everyone, and neither can you. If you have the privilege of getting bad reviews, you're in incredibly good company. No artist in history has made a universally liked piece of work; you are not about to be the exception.

WHEN I FIRST JOINED INSTAGRAM, I BLOCKED LITERALLY EVERYONE I KNEW BECAUSE I NEEDED THE SPACE TO EVOLVE INTO SOMETHING NO ONE EXPECTED OF ME. I NEEDED SPACE TO BE CRINGE. I NEEDED SPACE TO BECOME AN ARTIST.

INTENTIONALLY MAKE SOMETHING ALIENATING

Instead of making crappy art, try making alienating, divisive art. Make something you know your partner would hate. Use their least favourite colours, or write a short story in your sister's most hated genre. Does your bestie hate black-and-white photos? Make them a series. Get used to the feeling of making art that will provoke discomfort. It doesn't need to be mean or actually offensive! Just not to their taste. You don't even have to share it. In fact, maybe don't if you really struggle with this. I just want your body to get used to the feeling of breaking the so-called rules. Rebellion is at the heart of creation, so you need to get comfy with provocation.

ASK YOURSELF: *WHOSE LENS AM I LOOKING THROUGH?*

When you worry about your art offending people, ask yourself: *Whose lens am I looking at this through? Is it my own? Is it the imagined lens of my worst critic?* It could be a good note to have on your laptop or above your easel. You need to recognise when you're trying to perceive your art through someone else's eyes. You also need to start realising that these lenses you use to assess whether your art is acceptable are imagined. You don't know what your old teacher would think of this work; you can only imagine. And while we artists are very good imaginers, we are not omniscient. Stay alert to how you perceive your own art, and if you find yourself constantly in the imagined mind of someone else, call yourself home. This is YOUR art. It isn't for them. Their lens, in so many ways, literally doesn't matter at all.

MAKING ART IS DANGEROUS

Writing the memoir with all the bits about your mum, painting the nudes, making the music that tells the story of your abuse, these things feel incredibly dangerous. Because they are.

Just as there are consequences to people-pleasing art, there are consequences for courageous art. There are consequences for simply daring to commit to your creativity. Just being seen to prioritise your art can trigger an array of emotions and upset in the people around you. I cannot pretend that this isn't dangerous – it is. You are not cowardly for struggling with this. Making art is one of the most vulnerable things humans do. Making art is political and sensitive and often controversial. Many of the stories you've told yourself about why you should stay quiet are there for valid reasons. It's important to find ways to allow yourself to feel as safe as possible as you create, but it will never be without risk. Again, that is the very nature of art.

The point is that, despite those risks, making vulnerable art that is true to yourself is still worth it. I promise you.

My first novel, *The Rules Upheld by No One*, was a story about a sixteenth-century lady who gets shoved off to a nunnery, finds a wooden dildo (historically accurate), has a love affair with a fellow sister, and then finds herself in sex work. It was a story that reflected my journey with the church and my own sexuality. It is intimate. It is revealing. I am exposed. (There's no hiding in art, even when it's fiction.) This was a dangerous story for me to tell. I was doing the brave and vulnerable thing in publishing this novel, and even though it was inherently unsafe, I did things and took precautions to give myself elements of safety and security as I did the hard thing and exposed myself.

First of all, I sent an email to my parents before they read it. I just went inbox diving and found it for you:

> I wanted to explain why I haven't sent you the book earlier. A few things. First of all, it's pretty explicit and very focused on the historical research I did on medieval sexuality / sex work / pornography, etc. But more than that, I really didn't want either of you to read too far into it. There is no correlation between you and the parents, who are horrible. And while I did use my own experience with sexuality and religion to write this, it is not a reflection of my own upbringing or story. If you want to talk about any of it, I'm really happy to.

I wrote a similar letter to my grandfather who wanted to read it, and though I know through the cousin grapevine that he did NOT like the book and I've thought multiple times about asking for his opinion and filming it for what would surely be a viral TikTok, I choose, for my own peace of mind and mental health, not to ask questions about it.

There are many protocols to take, many boundaries to put in place, that can protect you from adverse reactions to your art. You should take them. Any safety measure that will allow you to take up space and make the art you WANT to make is worth taking. Create under a fake name. Write letters. Get legal protection. Have a boundary that says you don't look at reviews. Don't have comments enabled on social media. Tell people that you won't discuss it further. Whatever you need. Do it. As long as you make the art you need to make, uncensored and unapologetic. When we take the time to put in place these precautions, we get to create the art we were put on this earth to make. We get to be seen. We get to fulfil our creative potential.

WHEN IT'S JUST NOT WORTH IT

Sometimes, the price will be too high. The huge feud it would create in your family is not worth it to you right now. Your nervous system couldn't handle the upset from your audience; your mental health is not stable enough to have your entire church pissed at you. Remember, you are the artist; you get to decide. You are always the authority on this journey. You call the shots.

I occasionally hold back thoughts on social media because they're not important enough to me to share, and I know they'd kick up a fuss in the comments section. I weigh the pros and cons and choose to put my creative energy toward something else. Notice if you find yourself choosing silence too often, but know that you get to choose. Always.

SELF-CENSORSHIP BY AVOIDING CRINGE

I want to spend some time looking at how many of us alter and censor our art for fear of looking a little bit silly. A bit 'cringe'. Let's start off by defining *cringe*. It's acute embarrassment. It's what happens when you watch the *Office* episode 'Scott's Tots' or see someone slip when they're walking in public. It's the reaction, developed over a thousand generations, where we think something might get us kicked out of the community. The fear of being cringe stops many of us from developing as artists.

Whether you are learning or you are a long way down the road, you need to be comfortable looking silly. And if you want to be connected with any kind of audience, you're going to have look silly publicly from time to time. If you won't risk looking silly, the consequence is stagnancy. It's too hard to get better without being cringe. We don't improve as creatives without experimenting, and experimentation nearly always requires some sort of silliness. People would rather not create art at all than have people judge them for being a bit strange.

The very act of making art feels embarrassing for a lot of us. Especially when you are first starting out. You worry that you are being too indulgent, too presumptive, too amateur. That what you are doing is not brave but foolish and delusional. You don't start because you're worried people will see your attempt to even try as cringe. But if you never start, you can't ever get to the point where what you're doing is so obviously cool that you can do it with real confidence. So the fear of being embarrassed stops creatives before they start.

In particular, I worry we lose a lot of male and masc artists because of social conditioning around what art they are allowed to make. The men who want to dance, knit, write poetry have been told these are feminine things to do, and involving yourself in them would risk you being thrown out of the community. How much better would the world be if we had more male poets, dancers and knitters? We lose so much.

Similarly, I know we must grieve the art of women who do not want to be exposed to comments on their bodies or be accused of being 'showy' or 'look-

IF YOU WON'T RISK LOOKING A LITTLE BIT SILLY, THE CONSEQUENCE IS STAGNANCY. IT'S IMPOSSIBLE TO IMPROVE AS AN ARTIST WITHOUT FEELING SILLY.

ing for attention'. These gendered stories stop us from creating and sharing art. Not to mention those who fit no binaries, who have been discriminated against for centuries. Their experiences go far beyond protecting themselves from being cringe. These creatives are sacrificing their art to protect themselves from physical and mental harm.

Artists give up an integral part of who they are to be socially acceptable. You say things like 'Oh, yeah, I doodle sometimes, but I wouldn't call myself an artist' or 'Yes, I've written a two-hundred-thousand-word fantasy novel, but it's just something I do on the side. I'm not that into it' because you think that being seen trying is embarrassing. But it is not your job to be socially acceptable. Artists are meant to be the odd ones. You are meant to make people a little uncomfortable. You are meant to take up space in a way that makes people whisper, 'Gosh, what gives them the right to do that?' When they whisper those words, what they are really asking is this: *Am I allowed to do that?* You are a permission giver. You lead the way. Your impact goes beyond the art you make and carves out space for other people to consider themselves creative.

Without a doubt, people close to me have watched my journey as a writer and thought, *Oh God no, stop.* But more importantly, the vulnerability and visibility of my art has also provoked huge conversations with friends and family. My public dedication to art has made people uncomfortable, and then, for some, it has led to their own creative awakening. Sure, some people still think I should really keep things to myself. But for others, my embarrassingly public creative journey served as permission for them to start taking up space.

When you feel cringe, you are doing something incredibly right. You are testing the boundaries that have been placed on you to keep you small and obedient. You are giving permission to those who want to do the same. You are leading the way.

NO ONE CARES

It's very hard to lean into being cringe because you are wired to stay away from looking silly. As you embrace your strange side and create art that makes people uncomfortable, it can help to meditate on this: No one actually cares. Sure, a few people might make some snide remarks. But they don't really care about the art you're making. No one does, not really. They aren't staying up into the wee hours thinking about how you're going to that art fair where you're selling your paintings. They aren't getting distracted at work thinking about how you are trying to be an actor and how LOSER that is. You don't take up that much real estate in other people's minds.

This is a truly wonderful thing. The more a creative can realise how little people care, the more art and impact they can make.

Zoom out and realise that the video clip you posted of yourself doing stand-up isn't going to make or break your entire career. Zoom even further out and realise that nothing really matters at all, and you should do exactly what brings you delight and joy, meaning and fulfilment. To paraphrase Carl Sagan, you are a fleeting speck of dust floating on a sunbeam, so please make the art you want to make.

SELF-CENSORSHIP TO AVOID TROLLING AND CANCELLING

I've worked with and spoken to a staggering number of artists who refuse to share their art online because of fear of or experience with backlash, bullying and cancellation. They hoard their art, unwilling to be exposed in such a volatile space as the internet.

If fear of being cancelled or harassed on the internet is something that is holding you back from creating or sharing, I highly recommend you read a book I referenced earlier in this chapter: *The Third Perspective* by Africa Brooke. Her work has given me a feeling of power and safety as I navigate the online world as an artist. This space is difficult to negotiate. Struggling with sharing art on the internet is very valid. We need ways to protect ourselves and strategies to ground ourselves as we share our art online. I've been sharing my work on social media for over a decade, and this is how I keep myself aligned, safe and in power online.

I SHARE ART WITH INTENTION

I do not want to be in a pattern of self-censorship, afraid to share my art and ideas because 'What if they are wrong?' But I also want to make sure that I am thoughtful and sensitive about what I share with my audience. I do not want to be purposefully inflammatory to get attention, nor do I want to be insensitive. I never want to make cruel art. To ensure I stay aligned in these values, I have a protocol before sharing anything online, and it consists of two questions: (1) Is this generous? (2) Is this vulnerable? If I say yes to both, I post and can feel aligned and good about myself. Even if the art receives no love, or if it kicks up a fuss in the comments section, I know I posted it with consideration and in accordance with my values.

I ACKNOWLEDGE THAT, THOUGH PERFECTION IS OFTEN DEMANDED, I WILL NEVER BE PERFECT

'But that doesn't matter', I hear you say, 'the online mob will come and get you no matter how thoughtful you are about what you share'. You're right. A culture has developed that demands public figures and artists show up in certain and specific ways online. It is a culture of perfectionism. Problem is, everyone has a different definition of perfection, and no one can uphold everyone's standards.

I navigate these impossible demands by coming home to the fact that I cannot and should not try to make my expression so perfect it can't be questioned or disagreed with. It is an impossible task, and if I attempted it, I would never write a word again.

If you choose to share your art on the internet, or anywhere at all, for that matter, you choose to be witnessed in messiness, mistakes and humanness, and you must accept that in yourself and in others. Nothing is black-and-white. That nuance sits at the centre of humanity, and so it sits at the centre of art. I cannot and will not be so infallible that I am untouchable. I am human, my art is human, and I commit to showing up imperfectly.

I LET GO OF CONTROL

After I let go of my art, whether that is the book in your hands or a simple post on Instagram, it is out of my control. There is a high likelihood it will be misinterpreted. My art is consumed by many different perspectives. This is unavoidable and beautiful. I cannot control the reception. I can only control how I share it, which is always with consideration and care.

I am learning, however slowly, that disagreement is safe, that misinterpretation is safe. I don't need to be understood in order to be a valid and worthy artist. Not everyone needs to like me for me to be a valid creator. It is okay if someone thinks I am not a good person, because I know I am striving for honest, open communication and a world with more art. Africa Brooke explains that 'misinterpretation [is] an inherent part of human communication'. I think the point of art is to have multiple interpretations. This is unavoidable. I will not always have the right words or the 'correct' stance, and that is very human, and I allow it within myself, and within you.

I HAVE BOUNDARIES

When you share your art online, you are allowed to have boundaries. You are not public property. People cannot walk all over you. People do not have unfettered access to you. Protect yourself in ways that allow you to feel safe. Don't leave the comments on. Have a private profile. Don't read your DMs. Block people. Don't engage with specific rhetoric. Don't use specific apps. Have rules. These people don't own you.

As I previously explained, everyone I knew used to be blocked on my social media profiles so that I had space to share art and become the artist I envisioned. We need safety protocols so that we can do the brave thing and share art. You don't always have to play on hard mode.

It is one of my most controversial opinions, but I think the internet is the best thing to ever happen to artists. I think artists on social media make Renaissance Florence look like a backwater. Artists, of all sorts, with no permission, can take up space and share their creations. I don't want you to miss out on the opportunity to share your creations because of the darkness the internet can bring. I don't want you to water down or censor your art because you're afraid of the retaliation you might experience. I want you to let yourself be messy and human online; God knows we need it.

I know it's so much easier to not be cringe, to make art that pleases your grandparents, to stay off-line, to stay safe. But you are limiting your expression. Your potential for joy. Your success. When you create without censorship, you sit in integrity. A life of integrity is a powerful and full life. When we take away self-censorship, important conversations happen. When we let ourselves be cringe, we let others be cringe. When we let ourselves be truly seen, others feel truly seen. This is the art that changes the world. You must dare to make it.

SELF-CENSORSHIP PROMPTS

These prompts are designed to bring the cringe into the light. Let's spotlight the embarrassment. It's hard to feel shame when we bring it into the open.

1. **What makes you cringe? I want you to reflect on this from two perspectives:** When do YOU make yourself cringe, and when do other people make you cringe? Notice whether there any differences between these two things and gently investigate what's going on.

2. **Detail a memory of being cringe or embarrassing.** These memories can so often live within us and unconsciously or consciously influence our decisions and the way we show up today. I want you to describe it in detail. Let's face our cringe head-on right now. No one has to read this, I won't ask you to share (unless you want to! Could be quite freeing!) and you have permission to destroy this after writing. But I want you to come face-to-face with the cringe moment in your life.

   As you do this prompt, I want you to remind yourself that you are safe. Notice the emotions running through you as you tell the story, name them, and then remind yourself that you are entirely and totally safe right now. You are in a community that supports you and all your eccentricities; you are not going to be ousted from the group. You are safe.

3. **I want us to begin to rewrite our cringe narratives.** In the last few prompts, we have begun identifying what WE find cringe. Now I want us to remind ourselves that we are safe when we go against the social norms. This prompt is in three parts:

   - Fill in the following sentence: If I were to [insert cringe action], I would be [insert fears, even if they're not rational]. Try to get detailed in the fear, really understand what the repercussions of being cringe are for you.

   - Then I want us to begin to rewrite this story. Fill in the following sentence: If I were to [insert cringe action], I would be safe and [insert all the possibilities of magic and abundance that could eventuate from your embracing the cringe]. Notice and write down any resistance you have, but keep coming back to that rewritten story, this affirmation, and write it over and over again if you would like.

   - Finally, I want you to write about taking action. Rewriting our stories in our journals is powerful, but nothing is as powerful as taking action and rewriting our stories by literally changing the way we show up. So for the final part of this prompt, I want you to write down some cringe things you could do this week. They might be really small, and that's okay.

It's time for finishing touches. It's time for a release date. It's time to let people see you. It's time to stop hoarding your art.

ON FINISHING

Now we are going to talk about finishing your art. We can be at the peak of our artistic expression, making authentic, vulnerable art, but it doesn't really matter if we can't finish the projects we start. Finishing is the point in the journey where so many creatives absolutely, totally screw themselves. You were so close. You'd really found your voice. You'd done most of the work. But you got entirely unenchanted by it / rage quit / forgot about it at the 80 per cent mark, and now she sits in a non-backed-up file called 'art project 69', the bottom drawer, the attic of your parents' house, the garbage can.

Sometimes I think about all the unfinished art out there and wonder at the beautiful futures that could have been, cut short. Too many think that starting is the hard thing, or that skill development is the hard thing, that once you've found a good creative rhythm, getting to that finish line will be easy! Alas, finishing is the peak of vulnerability and one of the hardest things to do as an artist.

Let's look at all the reasons we don't finish a project.

DECLARING THAT THIS IS THE BEST YOU CAN DO

Calling a project finished means saying that it's good enough. And that means confronting all your perfectionist demons, which, for a lot of artists, make up a large proportion of your little demon zoo. It is far easier to say that something went wrong or that you'll come back to it later than to have to announce that this is the best you can do. Unconsciously or consciously, perfectionism is the reason for a lot of abandoned projects. Finishing means accepting the imperfect.

As we've seen in the perfectionism chapter, in trying to protect ourselves, artists adopt ideals for our work that are wickedly unfair. Your high standards don't make your art any better; they paralyse you. They don't protect you from embarrassing yourself; they stop you from finishing anything, ever.

We had a whole chapter about this, but I will say it again: perfection cannot exist alongside art. We work in a subjective field where perfection is a literal myth. When you finish your art, you will not have gotten it 'right'. In fact, for many people, you will have gotten it 'wrong'. Go and look at reviews of your favourite piece of art and marvel at how many of them are scathing. That's not important, because whatever the haters say, your art will delight and enchant others. Your art will delight and enchant YOU.

You must be brave and face the vulnerable moment where you say, 'Enough'. You must be courageous enough to declare something imperfectly done. Messily complete. This might not have been something you've done in any other area of your life, but it is mandatory in art. It will feel unsafe and foreign, like you're doing something naughty. You may worry that your arse of an art teacher is going to come and find you forty-five years later and make a snarky comment. But they're not going to, and you are perfectly safe to declare it finished. You are the artist, and you are the only one who has the authority to call it complete. Anyone who disagrees is wrong.

I'm not suggesting that you have to say 'Done' on a project you think is bad. I'm just saying you need to learn when something is good enough. When the endless tweaking needs to stop. When it's time to let go.

WILL FINISHING IT RUIN IT?

Finishing a project also means potentially ruining it, another terrifying thing to face. Will the last brushstrokes screw up what you had done before? Will the firing of your pot mean its demise? For a lot of artistic practices, the final parts of your process are the most dangerous, so it's far better to give up beforehand, right? Again, I am asking you to be brave. I am asking you to risk mistakes. I am asking you to be an artist. This is mandatory, terrifying and important. We think that the worst thing that could happen to us as creatives is that we ruin a piece of work. But far worse is to never dare to see something all the way through. To withhold the satisfaction of seeing something to its end, whether you are happy with it or not, is something you deserve to experience.

I AM SO BORED

There's a pervasive belief in the creative community that art should always be fun. And if that is your belief, I respect that, I truly do. But with that belief, it is unlikely that you'll see many projects (especially ambitious ones) through to their end. If you want to complete longer-form or daring pieces of art, you need to know that sometimes it's going to be boring, it's going to be hard.

Apathy can feel like the most uncreative feeling in the world. It isn't hot. It is an absence of heat. At least rage or anger can be translated into something fiery in our creative realm, but apathy is an artist's kryptonite. It's one of my most common emotions, and probably the one I fear the most.

Apathy for your own art feels dangerous. It feels like an emergency, as though we need to take quick and drastic action to protect our precious creative project from this lethargic poison. I understand why we quit; better to abandon the art than let the detachment and boredom take hold.

But it is safe to feel apathetic about our art; it isn't a terminal condition. It is part of this process. In a world where we are constantly stimulated and have ample distractions, we are no longer used to sitting in boredom. My own body responds viscerally to boredom. Understimulation feels painful to me. I will do anything to squirm my way out of it. If my novel of the moment is tedious to me, every cell in my body is calling out to do something else. But over time, I've come to learn that boredom, like inspiration, is an integral and holy part of my creative practice.

It is in these bored and apathetic moments when we must rely on our habits, on the patterns that we built when we did not feel this way. This is when we can utilise strategies like the two-week reset and the rhythm it creates. The spark will come again. In the meantime, we must keep going.

Sitting in apathy can feel agonising, but take deep breaths and be present with it. Your body will learn that dispassion is not unsafe.

Your projects deserve to be seen through to the end. Stay the course, take care of yourself, but keep plodding along.

SHINY NEW OBJECT SYNDROME

Boredom often leads to two responses. The first is the fiery commitment to doing anything but the art itself. Our old friend procrastination, in other words. The second is starting a new creative project every time you become vaguely disinterested. *This project,* you whisper to yourself, *this project is THE project, how could it not be? It's the best idea I've ever had.* But, at some point, this super-duper new idea becomes challenging, it disinterests you, and it turns out you were wrong. *But* you have a new idea and this project is *the* project . . . and around and around we go. We never finish anything when we're always chasing the shiny new idea. This sort of chronic unfinisher is interesting because they are often prolific creators. These artists are always making art, but they are also never, ever seeing it through. They rob the world of their magnificence. We don't get to witness them, and they never get to marvel at a completed artistic project.

When the shiny new project calls your name, it's easy to explain why you want to begin something new. But, Creative, what are you running from? You must understand your triggers. Are you afraid of the boredom, are you afraid of disliking your work? Are you afraid of being found wanting?

We explain and validate project jumping by underlining the merits of the new project, but we ignore the bigger problem: What are you trying to avoid? When you understand why you are so afraid to see a project to its end, you can begin rewriting narratives and taking care of yourself in the way that you need.

CONSTANTLY STARTING NEW PROJECTS IS A SNEAKY FORM OF PROCRASTINATION. WHY IS THE SHINY NEW PROJECT SUDDENLY CALLING YOUR NAME? ARE YOU RUNNING? ARE YOU AFRAID? WE NEED YOU TO FOLLOW THROUGH WITH YOUR ART. WE NEED YOU TO FINISH. OTHERWISE, WE'LL NEVER GET TO WITNESS YOUR MAGIC.

I NEVER FINISH, BECAUSE WHAT IS FINISHING?

I want to talk now to people who *do* finish their art but can't admit to themselves that it's done. These are the endless tinkerers, those who procrastinate by editing/fixing/tweaking. These artists need to learn what 'good enough' means.

Before we get into tactics and strategies, I want to acknowledge that saying something is finished is arbitrary. There is no finish line in art, which is very cool but also very annoying. You will have to make the call. It feels weird because there isn't a corollary in 'real-world' situations. You don't run a 5K and yell, 'FINISHED!' at 2.6 kilometres because you feel like you're done. (Although, good for you if you can feel done with a 5K at 2.6 kilometres, I love this attitude.) You aren't allowed to decide when you finish your taxes, or when you've gotten enough credits to get a degree. Other people decide those things for you, and they are usually set in stone. You are always told when something is complete.

But art leaves the artist to call all the shots. How wonderful and terrifying. It is no wonder we have artists never finishing projects that are almost certainly very finished. We don't realise that the power to call it done is in our own hands, or even if we do realise, the power feels too uncomfortable to wield.

I just googled 'How do you know when your artwork is finished?' and the first answer says, 'There is nothing that needs fixing'. Google . . . please. Your brain will always find something that needs fixing. Whoever thought of that answer is actively harming artists. They are telling artists to keep going forever. There will always be another brushstroke, a better line, a neater solve. So what are you going to do? Are you going to work on your project until the end of time (likely not actually improving anything but just shuffling things around), or are you going to let yourself be vulnerable and say it's done?

Unfortunately, and paradoxically for many of us, the closer we are to finishing, the more we find 'mistakes'. When I finally declare that I have reached the 'final draft', I suddenly start thinking everything needs fixing. There's something about coming close to finishing that makes the inner critic hyperalert and paranoid. *She doesn't want me to finish! Finishing means potentially showing people! Showing people means being open to criticism!* So here are a thousand things you should do before you announce it is complete. We become worse and worse at judging our art the closer we get to finishing; the closer we get to finishing, the louder the perfectionist voice gets. So, no. I vehemently disagree with the Google answer. You are not finished when nothing needs fixing – if anything, you're finished when everything feels like it needs fixing.

SO IF THERE WILL ALWAYS BE SOMETHING TO FIX, HOW DO WE KNOW WHEN TO CALL IT?

Let's strategise. I use author/YouTuber/philanthropist Hank Green's 80 per cent rule. Green says, 'Everything creative I do, I do my best to get it 80 per cent of the way to as good as I can make it, and go no further'.

I love this strategy. Beyond 80 per cent complete, we are at risk of ruining it and taking it too far, or just going round and round in circles not making a difference at all. By the time you're 80 per cent done, you're too deep. At that point, you have no objective ability to tell whether what you're doing is making your work better. Up to 80 per cent, things are usually pretty obvious. After 80 per cent, you're not the best judge of your work.

To be clear, I am not saying don't write the ending of your book or don't add the nose to your self-portrait. What I am saying is you have no idea what 100 per cent finished means. Eighty per cent, for all practical purposes, IS FINISHED. What you *think* is an 80 per cent finished piece of art, to an outsider, will probably look 100 per cent finished (though not perfect; never perfect). As a writer, I know I've gone beyond the 80 per cent mark when I start changing single words, rearranging sentences and then rearranging them back again. It's not useful. There are no new ideas, just repositioning.

Some signs you need to call it:

- You're making very small changes to the same section.
- You rapidly go back and forth on whether you like it or not.
- You are consistently scared about showing it to people / having to sell it.
- When you tinker with your work, nothing meaningful changes about it.
- You think it's close to being done but not quite there. (I am going to bet you're wrong.)

GET LAZY

I am now a truly excellent finisher, and it's because I channel all my laziness into the last 20 per cent of my creative process. I save up all my *I can't be bothereds* and my *who gives a craps*, and I put them at the end of writing my books. My tactic for finishing projects is that I essentially give up. This is good enough. I can care until 80 per cent. Then I get to quit.

Permission to give up has been the greatest gift to my creative process. It has allowed me to let go of art with an exhale, with relief, rather than with tension and concern. I'm not sure how I made it happen. It wasn't there with my first novel and seemed to arrive sometime around my third. Most of us have been taught to finish strong. But I am of the belief that artists, if we are going to half-arse any part of the process, should half-arse the end. I walked across the finish line of two half-marathons. I saw the gates a few metres in front of me, all the cheering family members, and, both times, I stopped running and I walked it in. Because why not? I'd done all the work, I'd trained for months. Shouldn't those last few steps be easy?

I HATE IT

Artists will say they can't finish a project because they hate what they've made. How can I say this is done? It is evidence of my own incompetence, and

IT DOESN'T MATTER WHETHER YOU THINK YOUR ART IS 'GOOD ENOUGH.' STOP BEING SELFISH. ART IS INHERENTLY GENEROUS. SHARE IT.

every time I look at it, I am reminded that my parents were right, I'm a waste of space.

Making something we don't like is a difficult thing to navigate.

But, unfortunately, I still think you should see it to the end. Because while you are the authority on your own creative journey, the artist, the centre, the god of your own creative realm, you are also really, really bad at judging your own art. You are way too close to the creation to be able to see it clearly. And by the time you come near to finishing it, you've spent so much time with it, you just don't have a handle on its quality.

I find this realisation incredibly relieving.

Your hatred of this piece is far more likely to be about you, your relationship to yourself, the narratives you have about creative shame, your relationship to your parents, that thing that happened in year-four art class than about the quality of your work.

If you still refuse to believe me, and you *absolutely know* that this piece of work is crap (you don't, but for now I am playing along with your narrative), I am still going to ask you to finish it. At the end of the day, it doesn't really matter whether you think your art is good enough. Give yourself and your process the respect it deserves and see it through to completion. Finishing is a skill, whether we are finishing a piece of crap or a masterpiece. We need practice at seeing things through to completion, or we are going to get stuck in a pattern of never following through.

Finishing projects is not just the privilege and duty of the experienced artist. All artists must learn to finish, even if we are beginners, because this is an incredibly important meta-skill for artists – something not directly about art but that will help you nonetheless. Do you really want to be learning this skill when you have a tight deadline from a publisher? Or when a patron has commissioned a painting to be done in a month? Believe me, you are far better off doing the work on yourself before you turn pro.

If you don't want to be a professional artist or are happy making art for yourself, it's still important. It feels good to finish. You can't live with all the ghosts of unfinished projects clattering around in your brain.

WHEN TO GET FEEDBACK

Whenever I hit the 80 per cent mark, I believe I have no more trustworthy opinions on my work and that it's time for me to step back. But that doesn't mean I can't get support from someone else. At this point, I will go and get outside help. Fresh eyes. Eyes that haven't seen this creation dozens of times. (As an aside, this mainly applies to large projects like a novel, not Instagram or blog posts.)

Choosing who to get feedback from is a challenging task and not to be trifled with. We must be picky. We must be careful. Getting feedback from the wrong person can entirely derail a project and prevent it from being completed. There are scores of nearly completed pieces of art that have died an early death because of feedback from the wrong person.

There is a false narrative that if we simply give our art to anyone, the feedback will be useful! Everyone's opinion counts! *No, it doesn't.* Everyone's input is useful! *No, it isn't.*

Feedback is a powerful tool and can help you feel that something is finished. However, you must make sure that you are doing it safely. You don't want feedback to trigger a stalemate, where your art stalls and never progresses. Unreasonable or overly critical feedback can sink perfectly good projects. Protect your art.

A few things to keep in mind when soliciting feedback:

- Don't get feedback too early. Most people aren't used to seeing art in the early stages, and it's often not useful getting feedback on something so young.

- Don't get feedback from too many people, especially if you are a new artist who isn't sure of your own voice yet. Lots and lots of feedback is boring, confusing and overwhelming, and it will stop you from finishing due to the sheer amount of work it takes to go through all that advice.

- Don't take the feedback too seriously. You are the artist, and you make the decisions about whether you take their feedback on or not.

- Find someone who can enhance the best parts of your work and show you how to double down on them, not just tell you where you suck. Most people think giving feedback means absolutely eviscerating your work with criticism. I'm not sure why so many humans do this. I believe they think it's helpful, but it's nearly always completely useless. Feedback is a skill, and most people don't have it. Criticism should always balance what is working with what isn't.

- Find someone who is used to consuming your genre of art! Too often sci-fi writers give their novels to people who don't read at all, let alone read complex intergalactic political dramas. The fact that they hated it and couldn't understand what was going on is not a problem with the book. At least, not definitively. What is certain, though, is that that writer chose the wrong person to get feedback from.

WHY IS IT EVEN IMPORTANT THAT I FINISH ART? NO ONE CARES ABOUT MY ART ANYWAY

Sometimes, finishing your projects will be about the generous act of making something for the world. But more importantly, and whether you are going to share your art publicly or not, finishing is about showing up for yourself. It is rebellious and powerful to back yourself. It is transgressive, in our perfectionist culture, to say, 'Enough'. Creatives who are in a pattern of constantly abandoning projects are in a pattern of constantly abandoning themselves. Seeing our projects to the end is something we do for ourselves. It develops us as artists, and it develops us as people.

This isn't about whether anyone cares about your art, this is about whether you care about your art and your creative journey. Finishing projects is a form of self-coronation.

Show up, in your own name, and dare to see it through.

TO THE ARTIST WHO FEELS THIS IS ALL A WASTE OF TIME: YOU CAN'T SEE IT YET, BUT YOU WON'T BELIEVE WHAT'S UNFOLDING. JUST YOU WAIT.

NO, YOU REALLY DON'T GET IT; I HAVE NEVER EVER FINISHED ANYTHING AND I DOUBT I EVER WILL

For those who are really stuck on this topic, we need to make it an easier game to play. Much like with the two-week reset challenge, when we make our goals teeny tiny, I want you to make a regular practice of finishing small things.

That means that the next thing you finish will not be the 150,000-word fantasy novel. It will be a 1,000-word short story. You won't be finishing the two-by-two-metre canvas; you'll be finishing the twenty-by-twenty-centimetre one. The knitted adult onesie is for later; for now, you'll knit yourself a small scarf. We are going to teach your brain how capable you are of finishing stuff. We are going to let you experience just how good it feels.

You might have big creative ambitions with huge projects on the horizon, but to get there, you must start small.

Make a tiny version of the big project and finish it. Do it again. And again. And again. You finish things. Make it a part of your identity.

Here are some ideas for how to shrink ray your projects:

- Instead of a novel, write a 1,000-word short story.
- Instead of an album, compose a twenty-second jingle.
- Instead of a life-size sculpture, make a five-inch sculpture using the clay you give kids.
- Instead of a three-act play, write a two-minute sketch.
- Instead of making a full-length film, film a twenty-second teaser.
- Instead of a full season of hour-long podcasts, create a five-episode season where each episode is unedited and no more than three minutes.
- Instead of a portrait painting, sketch a portrait one-fifth of the size in pencil.

To be honest, I struggle with using the shrink ray. I am usually a go-big-or-go-home sort of person. But for a lot of us, go big or go home actually just means *imagine* doing something big and then go straight home. We need to put our ego to the side and realise that while a twenty-second short cannot win an Oscar, it is a crucial stepping stone on your Oscar-winning journey.

This is how we learn to finish things.

WHEN YOU SHOULD ACTUALLY QUIT

It might surprise you after reading that spiel that I am actually a massive advocate of quitting. There are indeed times when it would benefit our creative practice to quit a project rather than hold on for dear life. Sometimes we must let things go in order to grow. Knowing when to quit is as much an art as knowing when you're finished.

From my own experience of abandoning projects, and my own work with many creatives, here are some signs that it may be time to move on:

- You've been working on the project for years and years and years, you are not close to finishing, but you're obsessed with 'getting it finished' before you start any number of other creative projects you have your eye on. This is common on first projects, especially when creatives pin their hopes on it being the 'best and only idea' or decide it must lead to their 'big break'. Creatives use a big, stuck project as a way to avoid all other art that is calling their name. It is a very good excuse not to create. Instead, you get to be stuck eternally. Quitting these projects is brave and makes way for more art.

- You realise that the project you are working on was someone else's vision. It was a 'should', a second-best choice, a project born from people-pleasing. You started this project because you believed it would be the sensible thing to do. It would get your teacher's approval. Publishers would love it. It made *sense*. The art you make should rarely make sense, and it should never be a should. Quit, and go and make the rebellious, weird art you know you want to make.

- You are a practised finisher. You have multiple finished projects under your belt, and you know that you trust yourself to see things through to completion. Your current project isn't vibing for one reason or another, and you trust yourself enough to let this one go.

One of our most pervasive cultural myths is that quitting is a major sin. That quitters never win. In reality, quitters are just people who have learned to say something is enough. You are allowed to say you're done with things. Quitting is so psychologically taxing for many people that they let themselves hang on way too long. If you have earnestly been trying at something for a long time and it just isn't working – and I mean genuinely isn't working, not the situation I described above where you can't admit that it in fact does work and is simply finished – you should stop.

I wrote a love note once that read, 'Your art is the cure to so many people's pain . . . and yet you keep it to yourself'. I need you to finish projects. You need you to finish projects. There are people out there who need you to finish your projects. Let's see them through.

FINISHING PROMPTS

There's some horrifying and potentially dubious statistic (it's one of those internet myths that sends you in circles looking for the original source) that says only 3 per cent of people who start a novel finish it. I see the same pattern playing out in all the different creative fields. We need you to be in that 3 per cent. You're here to be in the 3 per cent. Use the following prompts to examine your thoughts on finishing.

1. **What is your relationship with finishing?**
2. **Is the way you finish your creative work different from how you finish domestic or 'regular' work tasks?** Why?

3. What was your relationship to finishing projects as a child or teenager?

4. **What does it feel like to finish a piece of artwork?** Detail the last time you did.

5. **Make a list of signs that you've reached the 80 per cent mark of your project.** For example, you start editing small, intricate things; everything seems wrong; you obsess over what other people will think of it.

6. **When you ask for feedback, what is it EXACTLY that you need?** Detail specifics (e.g., I need a lot of positive affirmation; I need to know when they got bored; I need to know what they felt like when they witnessed X part of the performance or read X part of the book; I need broad-stroke feedback; I need detailed analytical feedback; I need feedback by this date, etc.).

DO YOU KNOW
HOW POWERFUL
I FEEL BECAUSE
I CAN HANDLE
FAILURE?
OH
MY
GOD.
I AM UNSTOPPABLE.

ON FAILURE

We finish art and now we must fail at art. Sorry. Most people would rather I not call failure *failure*. Creatives would prefer an entire reframe rather than settle into the surprisingly safe reality that sometimes we make bad art, sometimes we don't achieve what we set out to achieve, sometimes we fail.

When I share my own failures online, which is something I like to do at least once a year, I am inundated with people telling me that it's okay, they weren't truly failures, that I don't need to be so hard on myself.

You might have this perspective. It can be comforting to rely on platitudes like 'You never fail unless you stop trying'. And there's definitely truth there. You've been raised in a culture that wants you to avoid failure at all costs, and, at the end of the day, if you want to reframe failure as something that doesn't exist for artists, do it. But in this book, and in my life, I embrace failure. I don't shy away from it. I don't fear it. I know it happens and I look forward to it.

Failures happen. They do. No one is immune to them. Something won't turn out the way you want it to. Someone will think something you made sucks. Gatekeepers will reject you. You won't sell as much of something as you needed to in order to break even. This is failure. What you wanted to achieve was not achieved. But *you* are not a failure. You are just someone, like everyone else, who failed at something.

I have failed hundreds of times. I am not a failed artist. Failure didn't stop me. It didn't ruin my career as a writer. The ability to not only embrace failure but to use it as a launching pad for future success is a skill. If you can get to a place where you are excited about failing, you will be in a better position than all other artists. You will be more daring. You will be brave. You will take up more space. The path to creative mastery is littered with failure. It's how we get good. We hate to fail because we think that failure is the end of a story. That it says something true about our objective quality as an artist. It does not. Not only are you allowed to fail, it is mandatory. And we're going to learn to love it, together.

I'm going to start this conversation off with an inexhaustive list of my own failures so you know you aren't alone and you aren't a special loser failure:

- I've received literally hundreds and hundreds of rejections from publishing houses and agents.
- My first book, *Esther*, will never be published.
- I got the most detailed rejection letter ever for *Esther*, and my writing was eviscerated as 'unreadable' and 'stupid'.
- My first creative workshop had three attendees, and I ran it at a significant loss.
- My first merchandise line was only *just* financially viable, and we discontinued it after about a month.
- I paid thousands of dollars to record my fiction audiobooks even though they didn't make a profit.
- When I first tried Patreon, I had to shut my account down because it was so exhausting and made me twenty bucks a month.
- My first-ever course sold under a dozen units, and I shut it down because the hosting costs were higher than the income.
- The first season of my podcast had only a handful of listeners even though I already had twenty thousand followers on Instagram.

- I racked up tens of thousands of dollars of debt while trying to write my novel and waitress at the same time. I ended up having to ask my parents to help cover my rent and, eventually, move in with my in-laws. I felt like a failed adult.
- To this day, even though many people would consider me a 'successful' writer, things frequently sell less than I hope for, writing that I love gets ignored, and I sometimes forget to save enough for my taxes.

None of these failures were full stops. None of these failures were terminal. I was not a failure. These failures were and continue to be my teachers, my lessons and my stepping stones to triumph.

If we can get comfortable with the notion of failure, if we are able to look it in the eye instead of avoiding it, we can utilise it as a creative tool. We met psychologist Carol Dweck in the jealousy and comparison chapter. In her book *Mindset*, Dweck differentiates between a fixed and a growth mindset. People with a fixed mindset believe that their performance on a task says something definitive and true about them. So if they succeed, it's because they are naturally great, and if they fail, it's because they inherently suck. People with a growth mindset believe that things are more malleable. If you perform badly, you can always try again or learn to do better next time.

For people with the former attitude, rejection from a publisher or making art that doesn't meet an internal standard means they aren't talented. Full stop. For artists with a growth mindset, they might see the same rejection as an opportunity to get better at writing query letters or improve their craft.

The idea that you're better off believing that you can improve at a task is pretty obvious. The problem is most creatives aren't very good at it. Art can feel so vulnerable and personal. You might believe that other people can grow and develop, but not you. You pour your heart into your art; how could it not be a pure reflection of who you are? Indeed, according to Dweck's research, it's rare that someone has a growth mindset in every aspect of their life. So you might have a growth mindset about other things, like learning to surf or learning a new language, but not about your artistic abilities. I suspect that because art is so vulnerable, we're more prone to believing that a creative failure is a true reflection of our core being. We expose a lot more of ourselves when we make art than we do when we learn a new language.

But you get to become a brilliant artist *because* of failure. That's why this chapter is in the 'Building an Abundant Practice' act. You get to use failure to become a master of your craft and exercise your growth mindset. You get to use failure to find a joyful practice. If you can face your limiting beliefs, and your fixed mindsets, failure becomes fuel to your creative fire.

THICK SKIN

I've come out hot in favour of failure. And I am. Failure is mandatory and useful. What I am not in favour of is having thick skin. I detest the narrative that says creatives need to toughen up and cope with rejection and failure. Mistakes are allowed to hurt. Jerry Seinfeld says, 'Pain is knowledge rushing in to fill a void'. This idea is useful. The aim isn't to protect ourselves from pain. Pain can be an incredibly useful tool to learn and grow as a creative.

It is okay if rejection leaves you crying and if failure feels like shit. You're allowed to feel pain. This is your art and soul. You don't need thick skin to make art. The sensitivity of artists is our strength. We cannot and should not numb ourselves to the vulnerability of failure and rejection. I cry when I fail. I mope about rejection. I move on, eventually. But I always feel it.

I have a deep need to protect your softness. Too many creatives alchemise failure and rejection into a hardness, a bitterness. 'Rejection doesn't bother me anymore', they say, but the walls they've built around themselves in order to feel safe are impenetrable. They might not let anything in, but they also don't let anything out. Artists are soft creatures. We feel. We need that softness to create vulnerable art. Nothing breaks my heart more than when you calcify yourself in the name of having thick skin.

Mistakes, rejection, failures, they are a part of the deal, they are a sign that you're taking risks, you're doing the work, you're making moves. They are a sign you are an artist. Please, allow yourself to feel when you fail. You care.

Stop telling artists they need to have thick skin. Your sensitivity is what allows you to make such spectacular art! Let us be soft!

This is what we have been called to do. Of course, it stings when shit doesn't go the way you want it to. Feel it. Then maybe one day, when you're ready, you'll infuse all that feeling into more spectacular art.

HOW DO YOU PROCESS FAILURE HEALTHILY?

To process failure healthily, first, as we just discussed, you must let yourself feel. Suppressing disappointment, grief, exhaustion and upset is not the way you handle failure. That's how you harden and calcify. That's the way you cut off access to some of your greatest creative resources.

So feel it. Then ask yourself what sort of support you need when you navigate pain. Because not only do you need to feel the sting of rejection and failure, you also deserve support. Creatives don't often get the support they need because 'it's just part of the job' and 'they should be used to it by now'. It's ridiculous.

Athletes get injured all the time, and they have a team of physical therapists and rehab specialists there to catch them, hold them and treat them when they do. Hell, most high-level teams have psychologists on staff now to handle any major mental blocks. And yet, we think that artists should struggle alone. As if we are a special category of people who are meant to go through life without any support. For me, I need someone to just validate me. I need my husband to listen to me crying or being angry, and to validate every potentially unreasonable thing I say when I fail, when I'm rejected, when I feel unseen. In order to recover, I need to feel seen and validated. Rejection can leave me feeling foolish for even trying, so I need someone external to remind me that I have something very legitimate to give. Find those people. Online, off-line. Find them.

This is yet another occasion when we must sit in the artist's bizarre state of caring and not caring. After we have let the failure sink in and we have processed, grieved and gotten support, it becomes time to not care and to keep creating.

Creating is the salve to failure. Diving deep back into your space of authority, where you are the artist, is truly the most therapeutic thing you can do.

HOW FAILURE CAN MAKE YOU AN EXCELLENT ARTIST

Beyond handling failure healthily, you can use failure to thrive. You don't need to waste energy avoiding failure or obstacles, because you are at your most brilliant when you have to pivot, rethink and reimagine. Failure allows for iteration. It fosters a growth mindset. It allows us to develop as artists.

Creatives don't want smooth sailing. We don't want success after success. Failure results in creativity in a way success can't. Success can have us doing the same thing over and over again, while failure forces us to think outside of the box, and we thrive outside of the box. Really good art is made outside of the box. Iterating, rethinking and revolutionising what we do, because something didn't work before, is the way we excel.

Inversely, failure can also tempt an artist back to mediocrity. *My wild idea didn't work, better give the people what they want, better go back to basics.* Don't you dare. Failure is an invitation to push harder against the status quo, not to return to it. There's a great quote from Marcus Aurelius, grounded in Stoic philosophy: 'The impediment to action advances action. What stands in the way becomes the way'. Ryan Holiday's book *The Obstacle Is the Way* expands on this idea and helps you to weaponise it. To summarise Holiday's point and Marcus Aurelius's quote, we should get excited when we run into a problem, because it's probably a road map to getting better at something.

You don't have energy to create? Great! You must prioritise rest. You lost all the footage for the short film you were making? (I'm so sorry, please grieve this.) So you reshoot with more experience, and with a greater vision, and it turns out so much better. You sustain a foot injury during dance class and you can't perform for several months, but the rest you take brings you back to your poetry practice. Your failures are pointing to how much more powerful you can be.

You don't want success after success. Failure results in creativity in a way success can't. Success will have you doing the same thing over + over again. Failure forces us to think outside the box, and you thrive outside the box.

THE MORE YOU FAIL, THE MORE CHANCES YOU GET TO ROLL THE DICE

Luck will always play a role in your journey. We know that, for the most part, it's really hard to nail down exactly what led to someone's creative success. The only thing that is clear, and this will seem obvious but is often ignored, is that the more times you try, the more chances of success you'll have, the more your chances of rolling a pair of sixes (or a natural twenty if you're a D&D nerd).

The inverse is also true, of course. The more times you try, the more times you will fail. But who cares? Each of those failures means you ventured something. Each of those failures is a chance to grow and learn. The only thing that every successful artist has in common is failure. The longer you can stay in the game, the more chances you will have of either getting lucky or getting good enough to succeed. It really doesn't matter if you believe that success comes more down to luck or skill. Either way, embracing failure will give you more chances of getting where you need to go.

KNOWING HOW TO REPEATEDLY FAIL AND GET UP AGAIN GIVES YOU CREATIVE LONGEVITY

If you can handle failure, your creative career is going to be so long and so abundant. This didn't work? Doesn't matter, I'm doing something else now. You didn't like this? I don't care, I liked it, and I'm only getting better from there.

Failure gives a hardiness and longevity to your creative spirit. It makes it sturdy. Too many creatives play a short game. *If this isn't getting a response right now, then I am broken and I should stop.* But you are here to create art for your whole life. Stay the course.

GIVE ME A ONE-STAR REVIEW OVER SILENCE

Silence is a very specific type of failure. It can be the most disheartening and disturbing. No feedback to bounce off – just a feeling that maybe you are creating in a vacuum. You share your art, and no one responds. How can this sort of failure be useful?

I wrote this in 2017 and posted it on my Instagram:

> Sometimes it feels like nothing I do really exists. Sometimes it even feels like I don't exist. Because the novel I work on every day never affects anyone. The novels I've written before aren't touching anyone's lives either. They're sitting in inboxes, unread, stalemate. Or perhaps they're entombed in the rejected folder. The short stories I've sent out are in those folders too. Rest in peace. I wonder what's happened to my 109,848 unanswered emails to magazines and journals and creative workshops and authors and writing organisations. To all my reaching out. I am reaching out. Let me lead a creative life, world. Would anyone like to see me? What's happened to my phone calls, emails and follow-up emails? Did I even write them? Is my mail working? I refresh my inbox obsessively. I get tummy loops when I get emails saying my iCloud is full. I feel like every day I take a deep breath and I embrace the world, hugging it tightly, giving it everything. Then I wait, desperate to feel the world respond, to embrace me in return, to just wince at my touch. Acknowledge my presence. Nothing happens. Like I'm hugging stone. It's so easy to feel unseen when creating art, especially when we want the world to see our art. It is so easy to feel like what we do doesn't matter. Or that we are doing it wrong. I know that recently, I've started to feel like I'm doing something very wrong. I must be at fault. I mustn't be doing this right. Maybe I'm lazy? Maybe I am an idiot? Why won't the

> world wince? The funniest thing is that even among all this doubt, fear and deep, persistent questioning, I return to storytelling. To my words. She calls for me. And no amount of silence or nothingness could stop me returning to her. I persist, even when I sit in pain and crisis. I continue to create. Tomorrow I'll wake up, take a deep breath and hug the shit out of the world, she probably won't respond tomorrow, but I'll just try again the next day, and the day after that, and we'll just wait and see.

Silence was the hardest sort of failure for me to endure as a creator who wanted to make impact. It was so painful for me to feel inconsequential. I felt so stupid. But I endured. I tried again the next day, and the next day, and today I am sitting in a coffee shop writing this book, feeling the presence of my readers in the room with me. I feel seen, impactful and in community. I owe everything to my past self, the artist who withstood the silence. If you are navigating the quiet right now, I see you. I am so, so proud of you.

It may feel as though silence has nothing to offer. But we can use it to our creative advantage. Silence is not final. Whether it is silence upon launching a book, the awkward silence after you've told your friend you paint nudes or the silence of an unliked Instagram post, none of these silences are fatal. They don't mean your art is not worthy of connection. They don't mean you are not worthy of creative abundance. They don't have the final say. You just haven't found your people yet. They may be silent, but you must stay loud.

SILENCE IS AN INVITATION TO PICK YOURSELF FIRST

How do we deal with the concept of our voice being sucked up into the void?

Your brilliance must be validated and acknowledged by you first. You must love your work first. You must pick yourself first. You must be your first champion.

ALL ARTISTS MUST NAVIGATE SILENCE. ALL ARTISTS WILL EXPERIENCE SHARING THEIR ART TO NO RESPONSE. ALL CREATIVES HAVE FELT UNSEEN. YOU ARE NOT ALONE.

I told you earlier, in the self-censorship chapter, that before I release work into the world, I read over it – whether it's an Instagram post or a novel – and I ask myself: *Have I been vulnerable? Have I been generous?* I like to ask myself, *Am I proud of this work?* And if the answer is yes, then I ground myself in that fact. I give myself the validation before anyone else can give me validation. I pick myself. Then I let my art go. Press send. Press post. I release her.

With this attitude, the external response or lack of response cannot affect my initial response to my work. The work doesn't change in the silence; it's the same work. External response, or lack of external response, doesn't jumble up my letters or mess with the plot. It's the same work that I approved of before I shared it, the same work that I loved.

Granted, this can be easier said than done. But this is what I try to ground myself in. I cannot control what response my art will evoke. But if I loved my art, then I love my art. And I will keep making it and I will keep showing it, again and again and again. And if I keep connecting with it, maybe, eventually, someone else out there will too.

This is a lifelong practice, and it is a practice that scales up. It doesn't matter if you're sharing art with your best friend or sharing art with a million people, validate yourself first. You must be your first fan. Even now, as I write my first book with a major publisher, this practice grounds me. When this book is released, I will have loved it first.

DO YOU KNOW HOW POWERFUL I FEEL BECAUSE I KNOW I CAN HANDLE FAILURE? OH MY GOD. I AM UNSTOPPABLE.

Only those who can move through failure and keep creating find joy and success (however you define it). I am not saying, 'Do you know how powerful I feel because I don't get upset at failure?' I am saying, 'I can handle it: I process it, I grieve it, I learn from it and I keep creating'. If you can do this, you are a creative force of nature. It means that you have the ability to learn and grow. It means you can fail without defining yourself as a failure. This is part of your journey. It is your job to transform failure into curiosity, and curiosity into more art. Failure will be your catalyst for even more brilliant and prolific creation.

Failure will be your becoming. Failure will be the reason for your creative success. Failure will be why you become a creative master. But it won't be easy to navigate. As I type this, I am reeling from one of the larger creative screw-ups on my journey so far. This is really hard. I don't feel great today. But I can feel the alchemy happening already, the artist's tenacity taking hold. The 'well, *I* am going to go back to the drawing board and create something so flipping cool no one will know what's hit them' is settling in. And so, even in the depths of failure, when I am meant to feel powerless and silly, I am reminded of how powerful and brilliant I am.

I am so proud of us for making art, for daring to fail, for being in the arena.

FAILURE PROMPTS

I want you ready for failure. We are no longer avoiding it, we are inviting it. Failure is inevitable, and you will need precious and specific care when the inevitable occurs. Let's prepare.

1. **How do you speak to yourself when you have failed?** Really take a moment to investigate the narratives that pop up when you fail at something. What language do you use? What emotions come up? Physically, how does your body respond? I want you to write down the internal monologue that occurs when you fail. It might help to look back at a recent failure and notice how you reflect upon it (e.g., *That piece of art I shared on Instagram got hardly any interaction. I am a failure. I am losing my audience. I am clearly not doing it right. How am I ever supposed to make it when my best pieces can't get traction? This is so embarrassing. I should delete the post and stay off socials for a month*).

2. **How will you speak to yourself when you next fail?** Let us prepare. Because we will fail again. We will fail a lot. If we are going to find success as creatives, we must get good at handling the times when we don't hit the mark (e.g., *I honour your pain and disappointment. Feel what you need to feel. You do not have to ignore or push down any feelings. They are valid. You did a vulnerable thing, and you are allowed to feel these emotions. However, this is just another part of your creative journey. This is just another stepping stone to your success. Whether this is about the complexities of the algorithm or about the quality of my work, it does not say anything about MY worth as a creative. I am made for this. I am on the path. There are people out there who need what I create, but they may just not know it yet, and moments like these only assure me that I am on the path. I must be patient; I must recognise that this is a long game. I must continue to do the brave thing and show up*).

ARTISTS HAVE BEEN FED THE SCARCITY STORY FOR SO LONG THAT WE BELIEVE WE HAVE TO SETTLE, BEG, PUSH UNTIL WE BREAK. DON'T BUY INTO THIS BULLSHIT. ABUNDANCE AWAITS.

ON SUCCESS

We've discussed failure. Now we get to dive deep into the light and fun topic of success.

I find that most creatives, upon further inspection, are far more afraid of success than they are of failure. Take this seriously – it is incredibly important that you prepare for your inevitable creative success.

We all spend so much time rehearsing trauma, failure and worst-case scenarios, and so little time preparing for success. This is the artist's conditioning. You are taught to believe that the rug may be pulled at any moment. You fear that someone will laugh or not take you seriously. You expect a life of failure and poverty and scarcity. Artists are experts at reining in our dreams and lowering expectations because we believe that if we choose to be an artist, we are choosing a life of disappointment. Then, if we do find success, we are surprised by it. It catches us off guard and sends us into spirals of shame, impostor syndrome and fear.

As I said, I have worked with a lot of blocked creatives, and far more are stuck because of a fear of success than any fear of failure. Failure is safe. It is familiar. It is expected. Success has so many variables. It is the unknown. As a species, we trend toward avoiding what we do not know.

In this chapter you are going to define success for yourself, on your own terms, and then we are going to examine your narratives around success. You are going to recognise any ways you are self-sabotaging to keep yourself from success; you are going to prepare for the abundant creative future that awaits you.

WHAT IS YOUR SUCCESS?

When you see the word *success*, what does it evoke for you? You might have been sold a story that success means fame, money and big contracts with gatekeepers. But you must define what success means for you. Otherwise, you will find yourself climbing the wrong ladder, reaching the top and realising you don't want to be there. So much of this book has been about reclaiming the power taken from you as an artist. When you define success your way, you recover power, and you are back on your creative throne, where you belong.

I'm not saying you must let go of what your friends, family and the prevailing cultural narrative see as success – I just want you to actively choose your own definition of success. It needs to be a choice. For some of us, the idea that success equals money and fame will not ring true. For some of us, it will. Either way, it's okay. And either way, it's important to affirm that to yourself.

This work needs to be done now. You can't prepare for success too early; you can't jinx your success by speaking your dreams, you aren't being foolish when you decide what you will and won't do when you have a large audience. This is a part of being an artist. I need you to dictate and define the magic and abundance that is coming your way. I want your success, however you've chosen to define it, to let you be the most creatively fulfilled, joyful version of you. I want you to realise your potential and to realise that your potential is safe. I want you to sit on the creative throne and recognise that what you're doing is incredibly important for the world.

A WORD ON BEING DELUSIONAL

As we discuss defining success for ourselves, we must discuss delusion. *Delusional* is often an insulting and condescending word used to describe people with big creative dreams. Ironically, it is my belief that if you want to be a successful artist, however you define it, you must have unrealistic, delusional dreams. I want artists to reclaim the word. Artists are not meant to be realistic. Reality is . . . meh. You are building a world far better than reality with your art. Your job is to make the unrealistic realistic. Whether that means doubling the size of the sculpture you're working on or making a living wage as a poet – we must make sure we are not watering down our creative vision in the name of being 'practical'. Again, artists are not here to be practical.

Please don't mistake what I am saying. I am not asking you to take risks that put your well-being in jeopardy, but I am asking you: Are you taking it far enough? When I asked you to define success, did you rein yourself in? Hold yourself back? Feel undeserving and silly? I know it would be far safer to have realistic dreams, the risk of disappointment would be so much less, but you are an artist, and you are not here on this earth to rein it in; you're here to be exceptional.

WHY WOULD I FEAR EVERYTHING GOING RIGHT?

Now that we have examined what delusional and 'unrealistic' success could look like for ourselves, we need to look at all the narratives that are getting between us and our triumph. I've collated the most common fears of success and grouped them into the following four categories: the fear that success will trigger other people, the fear that success will corrupt your art, the fear of overexposure, and the fear of your own potential.

I want you to pay attention to any that resonate. Our fears around success often masquerade as other things, and identifying them is the first step to overcoming them.

THE FEAR THAT SUCCESS WILL TRIGGER OTHER PEOPLE

Many artists have experiences of success, especially when younger, that evoked a bad response from friends and family. Say you won a prize or your

TO BE A SUCCESSFUL ARTIST, YOU MUST BE UNREALISTIC AND DELUSIONAL.

essay got read out as an excellent example at school. Success provoked jealousy, being made fun of, maybe being called a nerd. In Australia and New Zealand, we have a cultural phenomenon called tall poppy syndrome. It's the idea that those who are doing well need to be taken down a peg. There is a veneration of the 'battler', the one who's always struggling. A lot of us, often unconsciously, have spent our lives trying to rein in our brilliance in case we get too good and therefore ruffle feathers. Or maybe you've held yourself back in order to maintain the image of the always-struggling underdog.

For those of us who have grown up in a culture that venerates the underdog and makes fun of the thriving, success can feel dirty or distasteful.

Though this could be a problem with almost any endeavour, there's something about being successful in a creative field that feels even more dangerous. Not only did you manage to thrive, but you did it with art. Artists are meant to struggle! What're you doing? Get back in your place!

You have been taught that success could lead to potential social ostracism, and that's scary.

Similarly, there are many artists who don't want to become too successful because they don't want other people to feel inferior. People pleasers are vulnerable to this experience. People who limit their success to make sure others are comfortable have often grown up in emotionally unstable households, where everyone's equilibrium needed to be maintained in order for them to feel safe. These creatives spend the rest of their lives trying to make sure everyone is okay, because that is how they remain out of harm's way. Being successful and, consequentially, making someone feel inferior or less than would not be safe.

But you are not responsible for how *they* react to your success. It is not your job to micromanage the emotions of those around you. Save that energy for making art. You can't betray your creativity, your calling, your audience in the name of keeping people around you comfortable and in stasis. It's easy to frame your actions as generous: you don't want anyone to feel bad about themselves or to feel jealous! You don't want to be the centre of attention or take up too much room when so many other people have so much to give. But in trying to be selfless, you are robbing the world of your art. You are depriving us of the opportunity to delight in you. You are also playing into the scarcity myth that there is room for only a few artists to be successful.

When you succeed creatively, you are not taking anyone's spot. You are not making it harder for other creatives who want to do the same thing. You are proof that creative success is possible. When you succeed and thrive, you give permission, you provide a road map to other people who want to do something like you. So many artists feel as though it is their duty to be poor and struggling, to be in solidarity with their creative brethren. I know many traditionally successful creatives who will do anything to seem like they are still struggling and sad, because of the guilt and discomfort of their success. They say things like 'Oh, but I work such long hours, you wouldn't want it!' 'Oh, but I pay so much tax!' 'Oh, but I have to employ so many people!' 'Oh, but my touring schedule is insane!' They are afraid that their creative victories make other people feel less than, but it is unhelpful and holds creatives back.

When you are successful as a creative, you are not taking anyone's spot. I will remind you, there is no limit to a raving fan's appetite for art. Remember, art is not toaster. You are growing the pie. You are expanding people's love for art. When you are successful as a creative, you have the opportunity to bring others with you, to make more room, to lead the way.

It is generous to be successful. This idea is so controversial and counter to what we've been taught, it feels hard to type. But I believe it. Do the generous thing and be successful.

THE FEAR THAT SUCCESS WILL CORRUPT YOUR ART

Maybe you worry that success will ruin the joy you have creating your art, that success will tarnish the purity of your creations, that it will mess with your motivation for creating. Success will make the creation process so stressful, you'll burn out. You won't have the energy for the output asked of you. You will let people down. You will become a sellout, giving the people only what they want and never making the art you really want to make.

A lot of artists really do experience all of these things when they navigate traditional creative success. Suddenly, they're working for someone else, they're making money for someone else, they've got deadlines, audiences. The pressure takes the magic away. It feels like an entirely different experience altogether. Because of this, so many artists hoard their art, or hold themselves back to avoid this sort of corruption. I understand it completely. Your art is something to be treasured and protected. For a lot of us, that might mean protecting ourselves from certain types of success.

However, I believe that you can prepare for your creative triumph in a way that allows for your art to be protected and kept safe, no matter the success you find yourself navigating.

Being a successful artist does not make you a public commodity. Getting contracts with gatekeepers doesn't have to rob you of all your creative autonomy. Just because you are well-known doesn't mean someone owns you. You must set the terms of your success before it happens. Otherwise, it's too easy to be used, to be manipulated, to accidentally fall into patterns, contracts, situations where your art and process are not protected. With the prompts in this chapter, I will help you to start implementing boundaries and decisions that will protect your art when success batters down your door.

Another incredibly common perception is that success breeds stagnancy. Success will force you to create the same thing over and over again, because that's the art that got you praise. We're back with the 'audience capture' theory. Successful creatives find it very difficult to pivot, even when every creative fibre of their being wants to do something else. They are afraid the rug is about to be ripped out from under them. *What if my success is taken away?* I fall into this trap every now and again. The other day I was rejoicing in the magic of my creative life, acknowledging all the ways in which art saturates my lived experience, and the next minute I was having intense daydreams about having to go back to the corporate world. *What if this is all taken from me?*

At the centre of this problem is the fact that artists have been told they're lucky to have anything go right for them; you should be thankful for whatever you can get. Don't ask for too much. Don't you dare have boundaries. Just get what you can get and be quiet. This narrative has meant that creatives become 'successful' at a terrible cost. We say yes to everything because what if nothing else comes up? We agree to the most unethical terms. We create the same thing ad nauseam. We aren't even enjoying our wins because we're so afraid they'll be taken away. We're doing what they want, not what we want.

Understand that you are the artist. You have power. You are the one who makes the things. Get clear about what you want and don't want with your creative life and fight for it. It is not asking for too much; you are protecting something precious. If you're already a successful artist, you owe it to your fellow artists to take back this space. If you aren't yet as successful as you'd like, you should be thinking about this now. Because once they start dangling the carrot, it might be too late.

The final 'corruption' I want to discuss is the most famous. It's the idea that money corrupts art. It is an incredibly popular, weirdly romantic story that runs rampant in art communities. It also stops artists from being remunerated for their creations. It holds us back from defining success for ourselves. I've had conversations with a lot of people who believe that art shouldn't be a commodity, that the very act of selling art changes it from art to product. I tingle with rage even as I type this.

I want to eviscerate the narrative that money corrupts art, but it is a sticky and old story. It comes back to what we discussed at the start of this book in the 'Small Magic' chapter. Art is romanticised to the point of being deified. There is a purity culture around the creation process that does nothing other than keep artists blocked and poor.

So why is this narrative so seductive? I have multiple theories. One is that people have an issue with art having an agenda beyond 'pure' expression. They believe that art cannot be true and virtuous if someone made it with the intention to profit. It harks back to the idea that you should make art only for yourself. If you make it for an audience, you tarnished the creation. God forbid that you want to make art that both delights people and benefits you financially!

Art is holy and spiritual and very, very human. When we create it, whatever it is, it will be filled with our complexities, our nuances, all our different motivations. You cannot keep art pure any more than you can keep yourself pure. Whether you make it with the intention to express pain, to feel seen, to connect with someone, to make money so you can eat and live, it's all art.

I also think that artists don't believe they deserve to both make art and make money from it because it would be too good. How dare we get to do something really cool, fun and meaningful and then profit off it? We see this narrative outside of the arts too. David Graeber, in his book *Bullshit Jobs*, theorises that we financially reward the more meaningless jobs in order to compensate for a lack of purpose. The more meaningful a job is the less we pay someone for it. The reverse is also true. Nurses, teachers, emergency workers all derive meaning from their work, therefore they don't need to be paid well. They were paid enough in good feelings.

It's bullshit.

Artist, if you want to make money from your art, you bloody well deserve to. Think back to act one, 'The Case for Creativity': art gives this world so much meaning, and you deserve to be financially compensated for that.

Your creative success might not mean making money with your art, and I value and respect this choice. But if you choose not to sell your art because you worry that money would mutate your creation into something corrupt, I need you to reconsider.

Your art has value. It brings value to others. And therefore, it is worth money.

THE FEAR OF OVEREXPOSURE

Artists simultaneously want to be witnessed and not witnessed. See me, please, but not too much. We want to be seen, but without the vulnerability and exposure.

We're afraid of losing privacy, being beholden to an audience, having to be present online, having people criticise us, having people watch our every move! What if you slip up? Say something wrong? What if people copy you? Steal your work? What if you get cancelled?

BEING A SUCCESSFUL ARTIST DOES NOT MAKE YOU A PUBLIC COMMODITY.

Again, these fears are not unreasonable. We've seen the horror stories publicly happen before our eyes. But we can't keep pretending we have no agency here. Just as we have power to prevent corruption with success, we are allowed to set the terms of our success. In fact, we absolutely must.

I repeat, being an artist doesn't make you a public commodity. You get to dictate the terms in which you want to be perceived. How do you want to be witnessed? Do not get caught up in the momentum of your success and find yourself living a miserable life. You are allowed to turn your comments off, you don't have to look at reviews, you don't have to perform whenever 'they' want you to, you don't have to release a book a year. I have no way of knowing this, but I'm fairly sure Beyoncé doesn't read her Instagram comments. I don't think Stephen King reads every review. Having an audience has its challenges, but you need to prepare how you meet them.

THE FEAR OF YOUR OWN POTENTIAL

The last section of fears is my favourite. I know it's weird to have favourite fears, but I think you'll understand. These fears are so revealing that once identified, they can transform your life.

The fears sound like this:

- *If I succeed, I won't be able to play small anymore.*
- *If I succeed, I will have to let go of my limiting beliefs, and those limiting beliefs make me feel safe.*
- *If I succeed, I will have to come face-to-face with what actually makes me unhappy.*

Success means you must show up. It means you must look at your addiction to struggle. It means you can't hide anymore. You must make the art. You must share the art. The realisation that we are avoiding the work because we are afraid of our own potential is huge. Realising you have something to give, that you could have a life that sparkles with magic, is intimidating.

Let me rewrite these fears for you:

- *If I succeed, I won't be able to play small anymore* becomes *If I succeed, I will get to discover more of myself.*
- *If I succeed, I will have to let go of my limiting beliefs, and my limiting beliefs makes me safe* becomes *If I succeed, I will discover that there is safety in joy, that there is peace without pain.*
- *If I succeed, I will have to come face-to-face with what's actually making me unhappy* becomes *If I succeed, I will discover what makes me unhappy and start a journey of true, profound healing.*

Success will mean discomfort. It does mean change. But it can be the most transformational, positive change you've ever experienced in your life if you wield it intentionally.

It's my belief that making friends with success is harder than making friends with failure. But we need them both on this journey. Most of us know failure, and it's easy to repeat the known. It's easy to prepare for the known. But it's now time to move into the unknown. Artists have killer imaginations; we can do really well in the unknown. How we think and feel creates our reality, and it's time to think about what an abundant creative life would look like. It's time to feel it now, before it's happened. Rehearse success. Rewrite the stories that keep you shying away from it. Know that it is yours and that you deserve it.

SUCCESS PROMPTS

These are some of the most important prompts in the book. Take your time with them, and take them seriously. Be delusional and unrealistic. You should return to these prompts again and again. Your definitions and boundaries around success will very likely change as you evolve as an artist and as a person, so it is important that this conversation continues.

1. **What is your definition of success?** This is the question I want you to go on a walk with, take to dinner and ponder over a glass of wine (or sparkling water, I'm not your boss). Scribble your thoughts about it in the margins of this book. Take time with it. To make the question more approachable, consider the following queries:

    - What have you been told success is? Think about what you were taught by your parents and by the cultural narrative. Does it have to do with academic success? A particular career path? A certain amount of money? Does it mean being always busy? Does success have a visual aesthetic like a certain car or type of house? Is success skinny? Is it dressed a certain way? What have you been taught a successful day looks like? Really investigate what stories of success have been fed to you. It's okay if you desire a lot of these things! That doesn't make them wrong.

    - What do you *not* want your success to look like? You might like to examine the lives of celebrities, icons or people you know personally who are deemed 'successful' but *do not* have the life you want. What about their success doesn't resonate with you? Take a look at the fears you have around being successful – do they help you answer this question? Is it reasonable to assume that your success has to have the same negative impact on your life?

    - What do you want your success to look like? This is the big part of the question. This is where you start dictating boundaries and rules around your own journey. This is how you protect yourself against the pitfalls of 'making it'.

2. **Write out what a day of your successful life will look like, or explore how success is already in your life now.** Create your own personal, detailed version of success. You may like to have a long-term definition of success, and you may like to have a day-to-day version of success. Having a daily definition of success empowers you to win regularly and show up for yourself regularly, rather than waiting and waiting for a future point of success. For me, this is hitting my writing goal of at least three hundred words every weekday. I might end up doing more, but if I hit that, my day was a success. And if I do it for long enough, my life is a success too.

3. **Make a list of boundaries about how you will show up in your success.** I'm talking about standards you will have for how you are treated, and how you will act if certain successes come to pass. For example: I never sell the copyright to my art. I never have a deadline of less than a year. I don't have more than one major project going on at a time. We are preparing for whatever success is coming. We are putting in place decisions right now that will protect your art and your art practice.

4. **Write down some of the stories you have been told, especially as a little artist.** Were you allowed to be unrealistic? Have you felt like you've HAD to be 'responsible' because of life circumstances? Did you grow up in a space that allowed for dreaming and hope? Were your dreams encouraged when you were little? Or curtailed? How have these stories impacted your creative journey?

IF YOU WANT TO CREATE SOMETHING EXCEPTIONAL, BE PATIENT.

ON PATIENCE

This is the worst chapter. Not the worst written (though you never know), but for me, this chapter is the hardest pill to swallow. It takes a long time not only to get good at art, but also to accept ourselves and our journey. We can be as good as we want to be, showing up, making art that delights us, the champion of the two-week reset challenge, even selling out stadiums, doing it all 'correctly', and still, we must be patient. No matter what stage of the journey you're at, things will usually feel like they're moving too slowly. This is the curse of the artist. Because the world has told you you're never enough, you want to rush to the next thing. Your first gallery opening, your first book contract, your next bestseller, or even just your first moment of true flow. We think that if everything could just happen right now, we would finally be okay.

I'm here to ask you to be patient.

During the beginning of my journey, I was told to be patient a lot. It takes a long time to get good. It takes a long time to write novels. It takes a long time to make a name for yourself. It was an intolerable truth. I had a specific and large creative dream, to be an author who got to write full time. When someone told me to be patient as I sat in my financial services job, disassociating from nine to five, it was really annoying. More than annoying, it felt dismissive and invalidating.

Motivational speaker, entrepreneur and bundle of beans Gary Vaynerchuk, bless him, talks about how insecurity festers when you don't have patience. I see this insecurity in so many artists. It festered within me. When I was creating regularly, in flow, on the path, I thought I was broken, untalented, delusional, because none of my art was connecting. But I was actually doing so, so well. I thought I needed to give up or do something drastic to 'fix' my creative situation (my situation being that I wanted to create full time but was stuck personal training / nannying / waitressing). But I didn't need to fix anything, I just needed to keep going. Time does so much of the artist's work when we consistently show up in small ways. We think that something is wrong with us and wrong with our art when, in fact, we just need to keep going. You are not a failed creative. You are not a bad artist. You are being impatient.

So, as we begin this discussion about patience, I want to speak to those for whom patience doesn't feel like an option. I'm so sorry you're sitting in a space that feels so intolerable. Momentum *is* happening. Life is moving. Things will shift. Creativity will change your life. Every single time you make art, you propel your life forward. A future version of you is looking back at the present version of you, reading this book, and they are so grateful for your commitment to your art, because you changed everything. I look back at the version of me who spent years and years in 'stagnancy', and I realise nothing about that era of my life was stagnant. Things were moving apace without my knowing or realising. One foot in front of the other. You might not know exactly where this creative journey is taking you, but rest assured it is taking you somewhere beautiful.

For the impatient artist, I see you, I validate you. I am you. Now let's talk about why we must absolutely learn to wait.

BEING PATIENT WITH BEING A BEGINNER

My favourite cartoon character, Jake the Dog from *Adventure Time*, says, 'Sucking at something is the first step toward being sorta good at something'. He's right. This world is wrongly intolerant and dismissive of the sucking

Shout-out to all the creatives feeling impatient with their journey right now. It's not wrong to feel impatient. It's not weak to be frustrated. I see you.

phase. People have very little time or respect for the beginner. A common reaction, after divulging to someone that you are daring to learn something new is: 'Are you any good?' It feels ironically unproductive to spend time on something you're not very good at yet.

It's a bit uncool to create art in your spare time if you aren't famous or successful. It's embarrassing to create and be terrible at it. So many of us give up or don't try if we aren't naturally talented immediately. Because if we're not good at it, what's the point?

Talent is highly overrated. It can be useful in school when the talented kid is encouraged, and that encouragement is important when it comes to committing and continuing the craft, but I also think it can be detrimental. Natural talent leads us down paths that are dictated by the natural (random) talent we have, without our consent. A lot of us don't love the thing we are good at. And that's okay, we don't need to do the thing we are good at. But when we choose the art that is calling our name, even if we aren't that good, we are making our own choice. We just need patience as we navigate the learning curve.

In her book *Mindset*, our favourite psychologist Carol Dweck suggests that far more important than talent is curiosity and the belief that your abilities aren't fixed. We come back to, once again, the growth mindset. This frame of mind allows people to stick it out through the shitty beginner phase. People who think that talent and ability are fixed are doomed to stop as soon as they encounter a challenge or setback. This is death to creatives. Because, as I've covered in the chapter on failure, challenges and setbacks are non-negotiable. But people who see challenge as an opportunity to get better, who get excited to meet with resistance because they know it is a sign they can grow – these artists have a long and incredibly exciting creative life ahead of them. The growth mindset means that all obstacles are simply an opportunity to level up.

So how do we tolerate the sucking? First of all – and this might sound like bad news, but I promise you it isn't – you will always have a relationship with sucking. Even when you're an expert, you will suck from time to time. Art requires sucking. It is a mandatory stepping stone to getting sorta good, or maybe even profoundly brilliant. Every time you make art, you strive for something. Every new project requires you to grow and expand and, in a sense, begin again. So sucking isn't only something that needs to be tolerated at first. It's something we need to understand and grow familiar with until we don't see it as a threat.

We must give ourselves the compassion and patience one gives a young child. When we impose too many rules or require ourselves to get good too quickly, we are going to make our creative process challenging and hostile. The chances of giving up become too high. Why show up for your art if all that happens is that you're a dick to yourself? Of course you want to quit; your working conditions are horrible.

We deserve, we NEED, to have an art practice that is underpinned by patience and compassion, but frustration will always be a part of the process. Frustration is a sign that we want more, and we are working for more. Don't be afraid of that emotion. It's safe. It's proof you're on the way. But frustration isn't an excuse to be cruel to yourself. You have high standards, that's okay – but being a dick to yourself doesn't speed up your learning process. It's going to slow it down. It's going to make this journey way more painful than it needs to be.

Art is a process. It is something we do because of the journey itself. Not because of where we end up. It's much like a puzzle. We don't buy puzzles, look at the box and desperately wish it were already finished! The point of the puzzle is to DO it. The point of art is the doing of it.

Behavioural economists Daniel Kahneman and Amos Tversky differentiate between the remembering self and the experiencing self. These two selves are often at odds with each other. Our experiencing self hates pain and hates hard things. Our remembering self often thinks back to the things the experiencing self hated and forgets the pain, remembering instead how accomplished and fulfilled we felt afterward. We are remembering it all wrong! Of course, there are limits. Some trauma is too much. But hard things, like making a film or writing an album, which might feel 'bad' at the time, usually end up as some of our best memories. We just need the patience to get through them. We need the belief that we are on the right path so that we can emerge from our struggle periods and be proud of the progress we made.

For example, as I write this sentence, this book is trash. I'm in the middle of the first draft and just dumping words on the page. It's painful. I'm frustrated. But do I want it to be over? If I could wave a magic wand and all the book's problems would be solved, would I do it? It would be tempting! Part of me wants that. The impatient part. But I wouldn't wave the wand. So much of the joy of writing is solving that puzzle. It can suck and it can be painful. It's also meaningful, joyful and fun, if I can be patient. I know I will look back at these impatient, difficult and sometimes hopeless-seeming months of my life as some of the best I've ever had.

We are now going to spend time looking at the specific aspects and moments of the creative life that require you to be patient. Yes, it's basically all areas. No, it never really ends. As long as you keep making art, you will need to keep being patient.

BEING PATIENT WITH THE EBBS AND FLOWS

Ebbs and flows come in all shapes and sizes on the creative journey. Sometimes we will create a lot, sometimes we will create nothing. Ebbs and flows happen with our income. (I know my tax returns look wildly different each year!) They happen with our love of the craft, as we undulate in our feelings toward projects. They happen with our skills, as one day everything feels easy and the next it's like we've forgotten how to type/sing/play. They happen with our audience, both in its size and in its disposition toward us. This journey is not linear. And we must learn to ride these waves and be patient with the troughs that *will* happen.

Knowing that the journey is up and down is the most important thing. You haven't done anything wrong when you haven't created in a few weeks or your income's gone down. You don't need to panic. You need to sit with the stillness and acknowledge that this is part of your art journey.

The ebbs and flows of creativity are not a threat to your safety or success as an artist. You need to trust the undulating rhythm of being a creative.

BEING PATIENT WITH NEEDING TO TAKE BREAKS

As a creative, you will need to take breaks. Sometimes they will be planned, sometimes they will happen suddenly without warning, sometimes they'll be short, sometimes they'll be long. These are all valid types of breaks. You need to be patient with yourself as you navigate time away from your art. You need to trust that it is safe to take time away from your art.

We can feel guilty, stressed and 'behind' when we take breaks, planned or not. But when you are not creating, you're still on the path. Life is artistry in itself. All moments away from your art can be fed back into your art. You are gathering materials. You are refilling the well. You are not wasting time.

In her book *Big Magic*, Elizabeth Gilbert talks about the concept that creative ideas will float away if you don't stake a claim to them. I agree with her, to a point. Ideas are to be taken seriously! 'It would be an honour to take you on and bring you into the world', we must say. We must write the ideas down and make plans. But I see so many artists rushing this process. *If I don't make this project right this moment, there's no point!* The dopamine rush of getting the idea is the only thing that spurs this sort of artist forward. An idea you had last week doesn't have the potency or urgency that a new idea has, so you abandon it. So many brilliant ideas are lost to time, not because the art was bored waiting for you to act, but because the artist let the idea go, deeming it an old idea, and an old idea just isn't worth the time.

We must follow Gilbert's guidance and claim ideas when they come to us, but it is safe to let them brew for a while. Your notes app is like a freezer; the ideas stay fresh there. Every idea does not need to be acted on right now. Your art waits patiently for you.

BEING PATIENT WITH GROWING AN AUDIENCE

You are absolutely allowed to make art for yourself. There are so many benefits to doing that (we saw the physiological and psychological impacts of art in the chapter 'Art Heals'). I also know that many of you create for an audience, and building an audience requires patience. You can grow an audience without patience, it's just going to suck. Without patience, you're going to want to take a lot of shortcuts, which often cultivate the wrong sort of audience and disengaged patrons: That guy who saw your one viral post, followed you and forgot about you. Fans who stick around for one album or one book. Rich people who buy your artwork at a gallery but barely ever look at it.

Building an audience patiently means building trusting relationships. These are the patrons who will buy your art and fall in love with your creations. These are your true fans. True fans are not made quickly.

Growing your community can take a long time. It has taken me ten years of very steady, slow growth to build my audience. My only consistent strategy has been patience. I turned up nearly every day and wrote a small blog post or note about creativity. Sometimes my audience would backslide. I really, really hated backsliding. This was, of course, measured by my social following, a notoriously bad metric for true fans. But the pain I would experience if I lost followers or felt that the engagement was down was embarrassingly potent. Over time, however, the true fans – the people who loved me and wanted to read everything I wrote – emerged. Those people listened to my talks, read my fiction, came to my meetups. It's not an exaggeration to say that for the first seven years I was writing, I had followers, but probably less than five true fans. If I had given up there, if I had lost my patience, I never would have connected in the way I longed to. In the five years since then, I've gone from five true fans to too many to count. I didn't do anything different. I just kept showing up. Sure, I probably became a better writer, grew in confidence, postured myself differently and had more work publicly available, but all those things were a product of the patience. All artists have long stretches they can point to when no one cared. They all found a way to be patient.

I want to give us compassion here. If you're frustrated, annoyed or impatient with growing an audience, that's really valid. It's a vulnerable journey, and we often feel powerless at the hands of tech giants, galleries, publishers, etc.

I also want to remind you that it might feel like you're backsliding or going nowhere, but if you are showing up, making, sharing, you are doing an incredible job. You are creating momentum. You are on the journey of finding your audience. While, of course, sometimes we need to change our tactics, I want to preach caution from chopping and changing our approach too much. Building an audience takes time, and sometimes we need to do the same thing over and over again before we get anyone's attention. That sort of repetition requires patience and faith. Trust. There are people out there who need your art.

BEING PATIENT WITH GATEKEEPERS

Anyone who chooses to engage with gatekeepers – actors who audition, authors who submit novels to agents and publishers, musicians who are looking to be signed, artists who want to get into galleries – will need patience. You will have to navigate rejection, form emails, grant applications, contracts and long-drawn-out silences. In these situations, we can't simply wait and wait, we must reapply and resubmit, make new art, try new things. It isn't a passive game. It is very active. But patience sits at the bedrock of all of it.

When we put our art forward to be picked by an institution, we begin a complex dance with luck. But luck favours the patient. The longer we can endure it, the higher our chances of being noticed become.

Patient creatives are happier creatives. If you are not expecting a response tomorrow or the next day, you become more process driven and more involved in the art. If you are constantly checking your emails, or expecting a reply in the next few hours, you fatigue, and you feel unseen, used or ignored. Patience allows for peace. And peace allows for longevity, joy, improvement, connection, creative fulfilment.

BEING PATIENT WITH PEOPLE NOT UNDERSTANDING YOU OR YOUR ART

Art allows us to understand ourselves in ways we could never achieve without creativity. It's natural, therefore, that we should want people to understand us in the same way through our art. We want our art to speak for us, to explain the intricacies of our human experience, to let us be seen and known. But art is not a mechanism through which we can force people to comprehend us. It doesn't work like that.

When you gift art to the world, you are giving the world a mirror. People will see themselves and discover things about themselves in your art. But it has nothing to do with you, not really. The moment you surrender your creation to the world, you are surrendering, full stop. However people interpret the art or the artist is not your responsibility. It has nothing to do with you anymore.

Your art will be misunderstood. More than that, your commitment to your art will be misunderstood. People won't get that you're speaking about your own trauma in a painting, they won't understand why you've used those colours that they think clash. They won't understand why you're spending so much time writing music when you're not even making money with it!

We need to find patience with our patrons and kin who commit to misunderstanding this journey we are on. It is not our job to explain ourselves or our art to them. They are on their own journey, and all you need to do is be patient with it. After all, you have important work to do.

HOW DOES ONE CULTIVATE PATIENCE?

Patience, for me, is inextricably linked to trust. My journals are filled with the word. I trust it is all unfolding. I trust that my only job is to keep writing and keep sharing. I trust that magic waits in the wings. I trust that my work will find its audience. I trust that my readers will get what they need from this book. I trust that even if 'it all goes wrong', something else is unfolding. I trust, I trust, I trust.

Creatives find it hard to have faith in a world that seems so unpredictable and so geared toward keeping them small. But these are the personal narratives you must rewrite, because when you do, you can exhale. I trust that my journey will not look like anyone else's, and that's okay. I trust that I can endure

I TRUST ALL I NEED TO DO IS PUT ONE FOOT IN FRONT OF THE OTHER.

the silence. I trust in my tenacity. I trust my process. I trust shitty art. I trust that I will show up for my art. I trust that all I need to do is put one foot in front of the other. I trust I can take breaks.

My lists go on and on, and when my trust is wavering, I repeat the words over and over again. So much is not in our control when we wield the powers of creation, but we must have faith that what we are doing is part of something bigger. We cannot micromanage every part of this journey, but that's good. It means we can focus on the art. It means we can step back and watch things unfold. Unexpected things will happen, hard things will happen, really, really incredible things will happen.

So while I still wouldn't say that I am a patient person – I have too much fire in me to be truly tranquil – I *am* a trustful person. I trust this journey I'm on, and I trust myself to be able to navigate what comes my way. I trust my commitment to art. And this allows me to exhale. It allows me to have an attitude of 'I must simply create and wait and see what happens next'. This approach slows me down in the best possible way: it lets me recline and breathe deep and enjoy this ride.

I'm going to leave you with some words from my journal entry marked October 13, 2021.

> Trust, darling. Magic is brewing but patience is required. Sit tight, make art, all is well. A creative life is unfolding.

PATIENCE PROMPTS

This big prompt is split into five sections, each question building on the one before. It is easy to answer these questions with the 'correct answer' (i.e., what you think 'should' be the answer). Notice if you are not being entirely honest with yourself, and get curious about it.

1. **What do you want now?** It might be a certain number of followers, a record deal, more time to create, a lifestyle, a role, a certain amount of money, fame, talent or skill. It could be anything.

2. **Why do you want it now?** This is not a trick question. There are no 'wrong' answers. I just want you to be honest with yourself. Why do you want it now?

3. **Would it change anything if you got it now?** It probably would! Detail it. Notice how it would affect you. If it doesn't change much at all, that's interesting; how does that make you feel?

4. **Are you on the path?** This is an exciting question, because it affirms either that we are on the way or that we need to take action.

5. **Do you trust that it is coming?** I am going to invite you to answer yes to this question, whether you trust it or not. I want you to affirm that your creative vision is on its way. That magic beyond your comprehension is making its way to you. I want you to cultivate trust in this prompt.

ARTISTS, CELEBRATE YOUR WINS LIKE YOU CELEBRATE JOB PROMOTIONS OR PREGNANCY ANNOUNCEMENTS.
THROW PARTIES.
DRESS UP.
STAY UP LATE AND READ BOOKS.
WHATEVER CELEBRATION LOOKS LIKE FOR YOU.
WE HAVEN'T BEEN TAUGHT TO COMMEMORATE OUR CREATIVE ACHIEVEMENTS.
THAT NEEDS TO CHANGE.

ON CELEBRATING

We don't have many social practices that celebrate artists' milestones.

There are no 'you finished your poetry collection!' parties. Nor are there any 'I finally overcame my procrastination and have been making art consistently for three months!' reveals. I would like to attend an 'I papier-mâchéd my own head and I think it looks great' ceremony, but I don't think it's ever been done.

So, alas, you must make these moments yourself. You must demand celebration. You must bask in your own brilliance. Unfortunately, you've never been taught how to do this. We live in a culture with built-in celebrations. These moments are ingrained in our social customs and are easy to celebrate. The birthday. The pregnancy announcement. The engagement. The job promotion. You have not been taught how to celebrate your own very personal milestones. You've certainly never been told how to celebrate your own art. In this chapter, you're going to figure it out.

Actors can be good at celebrating, so let's look to them for guidance. They have after-parties when they close shows and wrap parties when they finish filming, and as far as I could tell from my one season in a semiprofessional Shakespeare theatre company and my two years running an amateur community theatre group, most of them go out for a drink after every show. I think it becomes easier to celebrate when the celebration is collective. Actors in a play get to celebrate a group achievement. For the more solitary creative, it can be more challenging.

Similarly, with a play or a film, the actors have a real 'finish' date. The play is over! There are no more scenes to film! That was the final show! We will not do that again! Having a hard completion date gives an explicit window to celebrate. But for a lot of other art forms, 'completion' of a project is something that gets dragged out over a year and even at the end of that, did you really finish it?

When I finish a book, it's always anticlimactic. I know there is still a laborious copy edit I must navigate. Then a proofread. It's never really finished, and then when it IS finished, it has been a whole year since I kinda finished it, and the excitement has worn off. Add to that the fact that art never really feels finished or that we have complex feelings about letting it go. It isn't clear-cut, it's often drawn out, and so creatives forgo celebration in any form. Instead, we continue along our creative journey with no recognition of ourselves or the work we have done. It isn't healthy. We deserve more.

MAKING YOUR OWN MILESTONES

You must make your own milestones along the way, otherwise you will miss them, and they will zoom past you and you will never get to relish your creative ascendence. Instead, you will just wonder how the time flew by and be altogether confused about how you got wherever you ended up.

Artists are very vulnerable to the 'how the heck did I get here?' situation. I have finished books and have no clue when I wrote them. (Every day, five hundred words a day? Apparently? I quite literally forget this.) The flow state often leaves us memoryless of our process, which makes it even more important to notice and commemorate significant moments.

Artists are also very vulnerable to postponing celebration until they have their big break. Writers will celebrate only when they hit the *New York Times* bestseller list (and only when they hit number one, thank you very much). Musicians wait for their Grammy before they reflect upon their life's work.

Visual artists feel good about themselves only when they've had their first solo exhibition. You withhold the celebration until you are given permission.

This cannot be how it happens. It postpones joy. It eradicates and ignores your hard creative work. It is disrespectful of your process. You choose yourself when you celebrate yourself. Celebrating your milestones is an act of self-coronation. It is an act of power. It is crucial to the longevity and sustainability of your art. It's too depressing, especially before you get more external feedback, to never celebrate. It must be you. You must make your own milestones.

Moments I, as an author, like to celebrate:

- The end of every writing session. (This is a small celebration, an acknowledgment that I have won my day and once again showed up as the writer I want to be.)
- The end of a first draft.
- The end of what I call the 'full' draft (before a copy edit or line edit and after a structural edit).
- When the book comes out. (That one's the easiest! Because you get to share it with others.)

My celebrations aren't always huge. It's never a party, because of my introverted proclivities. Sometimes, it's a baked good or a glass of wine and a nice dinner out, other times it's a whispered 'heck yeah, I'm doing it' or a journal entry where I tell myself again and again, 'You're doing so well. I am in awe'.

In the prompt section of this chapter, I am going to encourage you to pick moments you want to celebrate. But I also want to encourage you to keep room for unexpected moments of celebration. Maybe one day, you figure out a creative problem that's been bothering you for years, maybe you decide to quit a project that's been holding you back, maybe you make something so spectacularly shitty, there is nothing to do but hold a party.

OBJECTIONS TO YOUR CELEBRATION

'A celebration feels a little indulgent', you sigh. 'First I make art, and then I celebrate myself? It's too much. It's too good!' But you aren't indulging. The world needs more celebration, especially of the arts. You are creating a world where creativity is celebrated. What is more important than that? Nothing.

'This feels embarrassing, I haven't even done that much'. Respectfully, you just made something out of nothing. Stop undervaluing the arts. What you are doing, and what you are a part of, is bigger than you realise.

'But I should wait until something actually big happens on my creative journey, like being picked! Or offered a big opportunity'. No, you shouldn't. This is the perfect opportunity to pick yourself before they pick you. This is self-coronation. You need to choose to make a big deal about this, before anyone else wants to make a big deal about it.

'But I just want people to celebrate me without my asking them to'. God, I know. But you have to teach them. Your creative world is so private and intensely yours, they will know what a big deal it is to you and what needs celebrating only if you tell them.

'I don't like celebrating'. Celebration can be whatever you want it to be. It can be a slowly and intentionally brewed cup of tea. It could be buying new paints or tools for your art. It could be walking the long way home. It doesn't need to be social, it doesn't need to be big (though it can be). I would suggest that, if you're having problems with this, your dislike of celebration might be more about not liking attention, or perhaps you feel cringe or shy about highlighting your creativity. This is an important thing to notice and explore.

ASKING TO BE CELEBRATED

When I got this book deal (again, there was no moment of 'getting', rather a long process with publishing houses that spanned many months, so I chose an arbitrary moment when I felt secure enough to know that this was really happening), I bought myself some expensive champagne, handed it to my

WHEN PEOPLE ASK YOU WHAT YOU DO, TALK ABOUT YOUR ART.

dear friend Pat, and said, 'Pop it, then say a toast to me'. He did so with enthusiasm, and I sat back and smiled.

I think most of us need support when we celebrate. I think we need to muster the troops, which requires a huge act of vulnerability. 'Hey, I did a thing. You might not really get it, but I need you to celebrate me'. It's sort of like how when we get older we must plan our own birthday parties. Send out invites.

A lot of us would much rather let the important moment pass quietly than ask to be celebrated. But resentment builds when we choose this 'easier' path. Resentment is poison to the creative process, it leads to bitterness, and I could write a whole devastating book about the bitter artist. Tell people about important things that are happening in your creative process. You don't need to tell everyone, just tell someone. Tell your online community. Tell a trusted friend. Tell other artists. Ask to be witnessed in this moment. Ask to be celebrated.

GATHERING WITH OTHER CREATIVES

As I write this, I am sitting with my Inspired Collective. We meet weekly. One week we talk about a creative topic, and the next week we create together. Today is a creating day. We are artists from all over the world, sitting in communion and making stuff. A few people are writing fantasy, a few people are painting, some are making content, we've got someone eating toast and another doing a paint by numbers. The community aspect of creation is healing. I say this as a raging introvert. I have a very, very small social battery. You can get me somewhere with other people for two hours tops, even when it's just my closest friends. But it doesn't matter how socially reluctant or anxious you are. Having people around you who understand the vulnerability of creating art is world changing. Having them there to celebrate you is transformative. No one knows the triumph of overcoming a creative block like another creative.

We need each other. We need to be witnessed in this dangerously lonely endeavour. Find someone who gets it. Who knows how hard things can be. Who can see you. And if you don't have anyone right now, know that if we were to meet, and you were to tell me about what you've been making, I would celebrate you.

I have a distant dream of hosting an annual artist Christmas party where creatives can come together with other artists and delight in the year's work they've done. Because even though it's so hard to celebrate myself, God, I would love to celebrate you. I want to toast you. I want you to get slightly tipsy and brag about all that you've managed to do this year. I want to eat with you, and just let the creative collective celebrate one another. I want to hear about what you've done, then grab the person closest to us and brag to them about what you've done. This event will be two hours and you won't know where I've gone every thirty minutes (to sit on the toilet and just breathe for a few minutes), but when I am not hiding, I will be in awe of you. Creatives deserve to be celebrated, and I want to spend my life making spaces for that to happen, because God knows it is not happening enough right now.

CELEBRATING PROMPTS

This is part journalling prompt, part party planning. We are reaching the end of this book, and I need you to take a moment to really reflect on how far you've already come.

1. **Choose at least four things you want to celebrate that are upcoming in your creative journey.** Write them down. You might like to put them somewhere public so other people can get the idea that you will absolutely be celebrating these milestones. I want you to write at least four, but please write down dozens if you can think of them. You might like to have two small things to celebrate and two big things. It is important

to recognise the fact that our creative journey happens only because of small wins, and they deserve to be celebrated too. Some things might be occurring soon, but you can also include goals that you'll expect to celebrate in a decade. If you have anything you need to retrospectively celebrate, put that down too. Examples: When you finish the two-week reset, when you finish painting, when you apply for a grant, when you do your hundredth audition, when you do your bare minimum every day for a week, when you do your bare minimum for the first time, when you do your bare minimum at all, when your pottery cracks in the kiln (hold some sort of funeral party in honour of its broken brilliance), when you get your first and fiftieth rejection letters, when you quit a project that isn't serving you anymore.

2. **Write down ways you like to celebrate.** How do you want to celebrate each of your achievements? You don't have to spend money (though it can be both big and expensive, if you want). It can be however you want it to be. For example, when I do my bare minimum, I celebrate by brewing a cup of my favourite tea, which I reserve for only these moments. When I finish my first draft, I go out to dinner at the restaurant I love. When I share my art on social media, I am allowed to go and buy the feta cheese I really like from the deli. I eat it. When I launch my album, I hold a tiny concert in my garden with my close friends. When I have applied to all my dream agents, I get to go to Spain, regardless of what they say. When I have journalled for one hundred days, I buy myself a fountain pen.

Some things to keep in mind when you are planning your celebration: There is no celebration too big or too small. Celebration is a very personal thing; do what feels good to you. My only recommendation here is to do something novel. I might decide to go out for breakfast when I have something to celebrate, but quite frankly, I go out for breakfast all the time and so it doesn't feel special. It's well worth doing something different to celebrate. Put in some extra effort. Recognise that this is special.

I also want you to notice if you are unsure of how you like to celebrate! Perhaps the only way you celebrate is how your mum likes to celebrate. It took me ages to realise that I hate birthday parties! And to realise that I would much rather celebrate my birthday with one person only. Make sure these celebrations are about you.

Now it is your turn. I can give you everything I've got, and I have a lot. But my celebration and belief in you pales in comparison with the power of your own celebration of yourself. Prioritise celebrating yourself as an artist. It will change your creative journey.

CONCLUSION

I'm struggling to conclude. Because, really, there's never an end to the creative journey. It isn't something you complete – it's a way of life. It's *your* way of life. However, because most people stop reading when the book ends, what do I want to leave you with?

I want you to understand how important you are.

How important your art is.

Creativity is responsible, generous and important.

The next time you tell someone you're spending the day with your art and you get the 'when will you be published' or 'why don't you do something productive like going for a run instead' refrain, I hope you know that they are altogether deluded and you are on the right path.

The next time you find yourself asking the muses to provide the perfect creative conditions, I hope you realise that you are the miracle you are asking for, and that you already have everything you need to make your art.

I hope you crown yourself, Artist. And realise that you are the creative authority on this journey. The sovereign of your art realm.

I hope you find your voice and fall in love with it.

I hope you finish projects and bask in their completion.

When you meet with blocks, and you will, I hope you find relief in the baby steps. I hope you respond to yourself with compassion.

I hope you rest.

I hope you make small promises, and I hope you follow through. And when you don't, I hope you are kind to yourself.

I cannot wait to hear that you made some very shitty art and that you had fun doing it. I cannot wait to hear that you made a piece of art despite the fact that your mum disapproves.

I hope you fail. A lot. And I hope the failures fuel you with creative energy and ideas.

I hope you realise that your creative journey is long and there is so much room for error.

I hope you chase the vision of your wild and art-filled future.

I expect you to succeed, a lot, in big ways and small ways, and I expect you to celebrate your success in big ways and small ways.

Art is your legacy. When your journey ends, you will leave the world with art, and there is no greater gift.

We need your art.

WE NEED YOUR ART

ACKNOWLEDGEMENTS

First of all, I want to thank my online creative community who have become my family over the past decade. This book is here because of you. I am so grateful for the way you have held me and witnessed me over the past ten years. You have supported me through rejection, failure, writer's block and depression. You have celebrated me when I got my daily three hundred words written, when I self-published, when I had a good nap, when I got this book deal. Every single win, big and small, I have felt your love and your support. I fucking love you.

MoominPapa, thank you for making weird, wonderful art, for honouring your poet's heart, and for showing me what unbridled creativity looks like ever since I was a wee one.

MoominMama, thank you for being my mama. Thank you for teaching me how to journal, for gifting me with the practice that changed my life.

Jonny. It would've been 2017, I was sitting in a random café in Sydney, bawling my eyes out over one of my manuscripts, rejected, defeated, incredibly depressed and alone. I was keeping my head down, but I felt someone sit next to me. There you were. I didn't even know you knew about that café. And you held me and loved me. I always feel your love, brother.

Kirsty, remember when someone paid me five dollars on Patreon to read my writing and I texted you and you replied, 'BABY YOU'RE A PAID AUTHOR!!' Thank you for being so proud of me every step of this journey.

Benny, thank you for chasing your dreams, and for letting little Amie have a front seat. You have taught me about the magic you can find along the way.

Amanda, my agent. Since I started writing, I have always said, 'God I would just love someone on my team who fights for me as much as I fight for myself'. I have found you. I am so grateful.

Ashwin – I am indebted. Thank you for seeing me. For contacting me. For fighting for my work. I am so grateful.

Laura, I feel so welcome and so seen by you. Thank you for taking care of this book baby, and for making me feel so at home on this new adventure.

Meg, this has been such a big journey for me, and having you by my side as I navigate it has been the greatest gift. Editors are artists. And you are a spectacular artist. Thank you for doing what you do and for championing this book in the way you have.

Isabelle, thank you for giving so much of your time and heart to this book. I have felt so supported by you.

Thank you to the extended team at Penguin Life, Ebury and Penguin Australia. I have felt so, so taken care of.

And Jamesy. At our wedding we didn't do personal vows because we both agreed, despite both being writers, that we couldn't put words to *this*. This magic, this creative collaboration of the ages, this love. And in a similar vein, it's very hard for me to acknowledge what you mean to me, and how much you contributed to this book. I'll just say, may this be the first book of many, many books we create together. Because, if I do say so myself, we make really good ones.

RESOURCES

Art is never made in a vacuum. This book is supported and held by so many other artists' work. I want to credit the books and studies I used below. I am indebted to your wisdom. Thank you.

Brooke, Africa. *The Third Perspective: Brave Expression in the Age of Intolerance.* London: Hodder Catalyst, 2024.

Brown, Brené. *Daring Greatly: How the Courage to Be Vulnerable Transforms the Way We Live, Love, Parent, and Lead.* New York: Penguin, 2012.

Cameron, Julia. *The Artist's Way: A Spiritual Path to Higher Creativity,* 25th anniversary ed. New York: TarcherPerigee, 2016.

Dweck, Carol S. *Mindset: The New Psychology of Success.* New York: Random House, 2006.

Fancourt, Daisy, Henry Aughterson, Saoirse Finn, Emma Walker, and Andrew Steptoe. 'How Leisure Activities Affect Health: A Narrative Review and Multi-Level Theoretical Framework of Mechanisms of Action'. *Lancet Psychiatry* 8, no. 4 (April 2021): 329–33. doi.org/10.1016/S2215-0366(20)30384-9.

Giblin, Rebecca, and Cory Doctorow. *Chokepoint Capitalism: How Big Tech and Big Content Captured Creative Labor Markets and How We'll Win Them Back.* Boston: Beacon Press, 2022.

Gilbert, Elizabeth. *Big Magic: Creative Living Beyond Fear.* London: Bloomsbury, 2016.

Godin, Seth. *The Icarus Deception: How High Will You Fly?* New York: Portfolio, 2012.

Gordon, James S., and Tatiana Znayenko-Miller. 'Transforming Trauma with Lifestyle Medicine', *American Journal of Lifestyle Medicine* 15, no. 5 (September–October 2021): 538–40. doi.org/10.1177/15598276211008123.

Graeber, David. *Bullshit Jobs: A Theory.* New York: Simon & Schuster, 2018.

Kleon, Austin. *Steal Like an Artist: 10 Things Nobody Told You About Being Creative.* New York: Workman Publishing, 2012.

Magsamen, Susan, and Ivy Ross. *Your Brain on Art: How the Arts Transform Us.* New York: Random House, 2023.

Mazzucato, Mariana. *The Value of Everything: Making and Taking in the Global Economy.* New York: PublicAffairs, 2018.

Pressfield, Steven. *The War of Art: Break Through the Block and Win Your Inner Creative Battles.* New York: Warner Books, 2002.

Rubin, Rick. *The Creative Act: A Way of Being.* New York: Penguin Press, 2023.

Shin, Jihae, and Adam Grant. 'When Putting Work Off Pays Off: The Curvilinear Relationship between Procrastination and Creativity'. *Academy of Management Journal* 64, no. 3 (June 2021): 772–98. doi.org/10.5465/amj.2018.1471.

van Leeuwen, Janneke E. P., Jeroen Boomgaard, Danilo Bzdok, Sebastian J. Crutch, and Jason D. Warren. 'More Than Meets the Eye: Art Engages the Social Brain'. *Frontiers in Neuroscience* 16 (February 2022): 738865. doi.org/10.3389/fnins.2022.738865.

Wang, Senhu, Hei Wan Mak, and Daisy Fancourt. 'Arts, Mental Distress, Mental Health Functioning & Life Satisfaction: Fixed-Effects Analyses of a Nationally-Representative Panel Study'. *BMC Public Health* 20 (2020): 208. doi.org/10.1186/s12889-019-8109-y.

Zardi, Andrea, Edoardo Giovanni Carlotti, Alessandro Pontremoli, and Rosalba Morese. 'Dancing in Your Head: An Interdisciplinary Review'. *Frontiers in Psychology* 12 (April 30, 2021): 649121. doi.org/10.3389/fpsyg.2021.649121.